Study Guide

for

Schmidt, Shelley, and Bardes's

American Government and Politics Today

2003-2004 Edition

James Perkins
San Antonio College

THOMSON

WADSWORTH

Australia • Canada • Mexico • Singapore • Spain • United Kingdom • United States

For more information about our products,
contact us at:
**Thomson Learning Academic Resource Center
1-800-423-0563**

**For permission to use material from this text,
contact us by:**
Phone: 1-800-730-2214
Fax: 1-800-731-2215
Web: http://www.thomsonrights.com

Asia
Thomson Learning
5 Shenton Way #01-01
UIC Building
Singapore 068808

Australia/New Zealand
Thomson Learning
102 Dodds Street
Southbank, Victoria 3006
Australia

Canada
Nelson
1120 Birchmount Road
Toronto, Ontario M1K 5G4
Canada

Europe/Middle East/South Africa
Thomson Learning
High Holborn House
50/51 Bedford Row
London WC1R 4LR
United Kingdom

Latin America
Thomson Learning
Seneca, 53
Colonia Polanco
11560 Mexico D.F.
Mexico

Spain/Portugal
Paraninfo
Calle/Magallanes, 25
28015 Madrid, Spain

CONTENTS

Preface v

Chapter 1:   Political Forces of Change in Today's World 1

Chapter 2:   The Constitution 10

Chapter 3:   Federalism 19

Chapter 4:   Civil Liberties 27

Chapter 5:   Civil Rights: Equal Protection 36

Chapter 6:   Civil Rights: Beyond Equal Protection 44

Chapter 7:   Public Opinion and Political Socialization 52

Chapter 8:   Interest Groups 60

Chapter 9:   Political Parties 69

Chapter 10:   Campaigns, Nominations, and Elections 77

Chapter 11:   The Media and Cyberpolitics 85

Chapter 12:   The Congress 93

Chapter 13:   The Presidency 102

Chapter 14:   The Bureaucracy 111

Chapter 15:   The Judiciary 119

Chapter 16:   Domestic and Economic Policy 127

Chapter 17:   Foreign and Defense Policy 136

Chapter 18:   State and Local Government 145

PREFACE

This *Study Guide* is part of a comprehensive instructional package designed to accompany *American Government and Politics Today, 2003-2004 edition.* The purpose of this *Guide* is to aid you in using the instructional package in the most effective and time efficient manner. The *Study Guide* will highlight the key features that the authors have incorporated in the text, to facilitate your mastery of the concepts involved, as well as, provide information about resources available on the **Internet** to enhance your study efforts. This total package should allow you to successfully complete your course in American government.

The Preface to the text on page xxvi gives an overview of the Special Pedagogical Aids and High-Interest Features, which will allow mastery of the key concepts of American Government in conjunction with the use of the *Study Guide*. I would suggest that you read over this section of the text very carefully before beginning to read and study chapter 1.

The *Study Guide* will provide an annotated topical outline to allow you to gain an overview of the important concepts presented in each chapter of the text. Following the outline will be a focus on margin definitions of key terms, which can be used to begin to assemble an understanding of the important concepts.

Exam questions will allow you to analyze your level of understanding of important concepts. The *Guide* will contain both subjective and objective questions. The subjective questions, short answer and identification, can be written in each chapter of the Guide to provide an opportunity to think about and process the concepts, and prepare you for these types of questions on examinations. The objective questions, fill-in-the-blank, true/false, and multiple choice, will be coordinated to specific pages in the text. Answers to the questions are provided at the end of each chapter.

A new part of this comprehensive instructional package is the *InfoTrac* feature, which provides thousands of articles to help master the concepts in the text. Study questions for each article are cited, and help students to focus on the most important points. An **Internet** web site is available to provide additional support in an inter-active format. This will facilitate answering questions in a more realistic examination setting, and receiving rapid feedback on your mastery of the concepts.

I hope that you find this Guide useful in maximizing your time and effort to learn the complexities of American Government and Politics. I wish you success in your endeavors, as it seems, our country needs more than ever, to increase the number of informed citizens, who will take an active role in the democratic process.

Chapter 1
POLITICAL FORCES OF CHANGE IN TODAY'S WORLD

CHAPTER SUMMARY

Political forces create changes in the way all of us live. The terrorist attack on September 11, 2001 has changed the American political landscape. This chapter will discuss some of the questions and principles that are fundamental to the American, and any political system. [p. 5]

Change versus Stability

The government is necessary to balance the forces of change and stability. The election system in the United States allows us to change the balance of power in the national government, every two years, if we choose. In 2002, most of the incumbent leaders in the Congress were reelected. [p. 5-6]

What is Politics?

Politics is defined by Harold Lasswell as, "Who get what, when and how?" in a society. The authors of the text define politics as the reference to conflict and conflict resolution in society. Conflict is always present in society because of three major reasons. One, the differences of belief or ideology. Two, the differences in the perceived goals of the society. Three, scarce resources exist, and not every want can be satisfied by society. By necessity, the government spending more on senior citizens will mean spending less on younger people. [p. 6-7]

The Need for Government and Power

Government refers to the institutions by which conflicts are resolved and values allocated. These institutions require authority, legitimacy, and power, in order to accomplish their purpose to resolve conflict. Authority is the feature of a leader or institution that compel obedience. Usually this obedience is become of legitimacy. Legitimacy is the status conferred by the people on the officials, acts, and institutions of the government. The people believe the actions taken are legal and right. Power is the ability to cause others to modify their behavior and to conform to what the power holder wants. To sum up, authority is the legal use of power. [p. 7-10]

Who Governs?

A fundamental question of politics has to with, who makes political decisions for a society? Anarchy is where no government exists, and individuals must try to resolve conflicts on their own. In an Oligarchy, a few members of the elite make decisions. An Elite is defined as an upper socioeconomic class. Aristocracy refers to decisions made by the best suited in terms of wealth, education, intelligence, and family prestige. In a Democracy, the majority of people make decisions. p. 10. Direct Democracy is where people make decisions in person, like the New England town meeting. A possible danger of this form democracy can be mob rule, in which the majority abuses the rights of minority groups. p. 11 This danger has led our society to create a Republic or representative Democracy, in which representatives are elected by the people to make and enforce laws. The three principles essential for democratic government in our society are; universal suffrage, the right of all adults to vote for representatives; majority rule with the protection of minority rights, and limited government, the authority of government is limited by a written document or widely held beliefs. [p. 13-14]

Do We Have a Democracy?

Elite theory has suggested that society is ruled by a small number of wealthy people, who exercise power in their self-interest. The primary goal of such a society is stability, because elites do not want to see any change in their status p. 13 Pluralism theory has proposed that conflict in society is among interest groups. Bargaining and compromise among groups determine political decision-making. Hyperpluralism has suggested that interest groups can become so powerful that the society is virtually paralyzed by the struggle between interest groups. p. [14-16]

Ideas and Politics: Political Culture

Political Culture can be defined as a patterned set of ideas, values, and ways of thinking about government and politics. The process by which such beliefs and values are transmitted to Immigrants and our children is called Political Socialization. [p. 16-17]

The Fundamental Values of the American political culture can be defined as: liberty, the greatest freedom of individuals that is consistent with the freedom of other individuals in society, equality, all people are of equal worth, and property, the right of individual ownership p. [18-20]. Political culture has been important in holding society together by persuading people to support the existing political process. The disputed 2000 presidential election showed the stability of the American political culture, as only 17 percent of Americans polled ever described the situations as a crisis. [p. 20-22]

The Changing Face of America

The context of the American society is changing as American's age, become more diverse, and need new laws and policies. Almost 13% of the population was sixty-five years or older in 2000. Combined with low birth rates, this has important implications for retirement and pension systems, including Social Security. The shrinking of the younger population is a worldwide event in developed countries. p. 22. See Figure 1-1 p. 22. Hispanics, African Americans, and Asian Americans have become a larger proportion of the United States population because of higher birth rates and immigration increases. p. 23. See Figure 1-2 p. 23. Other trends reveal that over 75% of the population lived in urban areas in 2002. Today, 25% of children live in one-parent households. National surveys have found about 20% of all Americans are barely literate. p. 23

Ideas and Politics: Ideology

Ideology can be defined as a comprehensive and logical set of beliefs about the nature of people, and about the institutions and role of government. American ideology has been dominated by two moderate ideologies. Liberalism is the belief that includes support of positive government action to improve the welfare of individuals, support civil rights, and political and social change. Conservatism is the belief that includes support of a limited role for government helping individuals, support for traditional values, and a cautious response to change. [p. 24-25]

America's Politics: Why Is it Important Today?

Today, what happens in government at all levels is more important than at any time since World War II. In these troubled times, citizens must be better informed, and must increase the level of participation in the political process. The discussion of how serious is the political situation, has produced debate about requiring voters to pass a test before being able to vote. [p. 25]

KEY TERMS

authority- p. 8

conservatism- p. 24

democracy- p.10

direct democracy- p. 10

elite theory- p. 15

equality- p. 18

government- p. 7

ideology- p. 24

liberalism- p.24

liberty- p. 18

limited government- p. 14

pluralism- p. 16

political socialization- p. 17

politics- p. 6

power- p. 8

property- p. 20

republic- p. 13

OTHER RESOURCES

A number of valuable supplements are available to students using the Schmidt, Shelley, and Bardes text. The full list of the supplements is in the preface to this study guide. Ask your instructor how to obtain these resources. One supplement is highlighted here, the INFOTRAC Online Library.

INFOTRAC EXERCISES

Log on to http://www.infotrac-college.com.
Enter your Pass code that came with your textbook.
You can access the article by typing the exact phrase below.

Ideology
"The Human Rights Blame Game"
This article discusses the conflict between the U.S. and Europe over human rights.
The U.S. Senate has refused to support the International Criminal Court (ICC). Both support human rights, but the U.S. believes in a Libertarian view that human rights are individual liberty rights, while Europeans believe in an Egalitarian view that human rights are social equality rights.

Study Questions
1. Do you agree with the Libertarian or Egalitarian view of individual rights?
2. Should the U.S. support the ICC?
3. How would you resolve this conflict?

Political Socialization
"Service Learning and Political Socialization"
This article discusses the concept of Service Learning, as a major tool in creating better-informed and more active citizens for the future.

Study Questions
1. Have you participated in a service-learning program?
2. Do you think this program should be part of a higher education?

Liberty
"Whose homeland security"?
Congresswoman Cynthia McKinney discusses her concern about an erosion of human rights at home, while U.S. foreign policy is selective in attacking African terrorists.

Study Questions
1. Do you think U.S. foreign policy has been inconsistent about terrorist activities?
2. Do you feel that laws or policies enacted since September 11 have eroded human rights?

PRACTICE EXAM
(Answers appear at the end of this chapter.)

Fill-In-The-Blank   Supply the missing word(s) or term to complete the sentence.

1.   All major definitions of politics try to explain how human beings regulate _____ in their society.

2.   2.The features of a leader or an institution that compel obedience are called _____.

3.   The ancient Greek city-state of Athens is often considered to be the historical model for
_____.

4.   The U.S. Constitution creates a form of republican government known as a _____.

5.   From the elite theory perspective, the primary goal of government is _____, because elites do not want any change to their status.

6.   In the pluralist's view, politics is the struggle among _____ to gain benefits for their members.

7.   A fundamental source of political socialization is the _____.

8.   Democracy, liberty, equality, and property lie at the core of American
_____.

9.   Immigration, as a percentage of total U.S. population growth, since 1970, has _____.

10. Within the American electorate, the two ideological viewpoints that are most commonly held are
_____ and _____.

True/False   Circle the appropriate letter to indicate if the statement is true or false.

T   F   1.   Political scientists are able to agree that politics involves the resolution of social Conflict.

T   F   2.   In democratic nations, most citizens comply with the law because they accept the authority of the government and its officials.

T   F   3.   Direct democracy in ancient Athens was considered to have been the ideal form of democracy.

T   F   4.   James Madison was a strong advocate of a "pure democracy" for the American political system.

T   F   5.   In a representative democracy, the people hold the ultimate power over the government through the election process.

T   F   6.   The elite perspective sees the mass population as active and involved in the decisions of government.

T   F   7.   A democratic system paralyzed by the struggle between interest groups is called Hyperpluralism.

T   F   8.   The basic guarantee of liberties for citizens within the American political system is found in the body of the U.S. Constitution.

T   F   9.   The 2000 census indicates a very low rate of U.S. population growth.

T   F   10. Immigrants are likely to shape American politics in the future.

Multiple choice   Circle the correct response.

1. All definition of politics try to explain how human beings regulate
    a. Natural resources within their society
    b. Good and evil within a complex society
    c. Self-expression
    d. Conflict within their society

2. A form of government in which every aspect of political, social, and economic life is controlled by the government is called a(n)
    a. Democratic regime
    b. Socialist regime
    c. Totalitarian regime
    d. Oligarchy

3. When each individual makes his or her own rules for behavior and there are no laws and no government
    a. Pure democracy prevails
    b. Anarchy exists
    c. An oligarchy exists
    d. The ideal form of government prevails

4. The Athenian model of government was considered
    a. The ideal form of direct democracy
    b. A weak and ineffective form of government
    c. The reason the Roman legions were able to conquer Greece
    d. The forerunner of communism

5. Initiative is a procedure by which voters can
    a. Directly make laws
    b. Remove elected officials
    c. Propose a law or constitutional amendment
    d. Place candidates on a ballot

6. The U.S. Constitution creates a form of republican government known as a
    a. Pure democracy
    b. Confederation
    c. Representative democracy
    d. Majoritarian system

7. A central feature to the American governmental system is
    a. The supremacy of Congress over the other branches
    b. Control of the airwaves
    c. The tendency to provide foreign aid to every country
    d. Equality of every individual before the law

8. To ensure that majority rule does not become oppressive, modern democracies
    a. Provide guarantees of minority rights
    b. Have constitutions that are difficult to amend
    c. Use plurality voting for most decisions
    d. Hold free, competitive elections

9. The U.S. Constitution
    a. Does not set forth enough detail as to how the government should function
    b. Is too open to interpretation, which creates confusion for government leaders
    c. Has more amendments than any other national constitution
    d. Set forth the fundamental structure of the government and the limits to its power

10. According to the elite perspective, the primary goal of government should be stability, because
    a. Elites do not want any change in their status
    b. Stability is the only thing that can ensure a good life
    c. Instability will create greater welfare problems
    d. Unstable government is more vulnerable to foreign invasion

11. Pluralist theory believes that decisions are made in American politics by
    a. The mass population
    b. The governing elites
    c. The wealthy
    d. The competition between groups trying to gain benefits for their members

12. When group needs control government decision-making to the detriment of the general population, we have a condition known as
    a. Legislative fiat
    b. Democratization of groups
    c. Hyperpluralism
    d. Factionalism

13. The pattern of political beliefs and values characteristics of a community or population is referred to as
    a. Public opinion
    b. Democratic heritage
    c. Political culture
    d. Consensus of opinion

14. The process by which Americans come to accept a single set of values concerning the Political system is called
    a. Enculturation
    b. Education
    c. Political socialization
    d. Propaganda

15. Democracy, liberty, equality, and property are
    a. Concepts that no longer have meaning in modern political systems
    b. Now thought to be unattainable in a modern pluralistic society
    c. Concepts that lie at the core of American political culture
    d. Concepts that encompass our entire political heritage

16. The ideology that believes the government should exercise the least power is
    a. Socialism
    b. Liberalism
    c. Conservatism
    d. Libertarianism

17. What do the author's of the text feel will bring Americans true equality?
    a. new laws
    b. a legal conflict
    c. each individual considering the needs of all others
    d. the Internet

18. The results of the disputed 2000 presidential election revealed the strength of
    a. the Congress
    b. the Courts
    c. the President
    d. the Political Culture

19. Which state is highlighted in the text as having a majority-minority population in 2001?
    a. Idaho
    b. Oregon
    c. California
    d. Texas

20. The number of American 65 years and older today is approaching
    a. 5% of the population
    b. 8% of the population
    c. 13% of the population
    d. 40% of the population

Short Essay Questions. Briefly address the major concepts raised by the following questions.

1. Explain the role of politics in an organized society.

2. Explain the origins of democracy and the different types of democracy.

3. Define the fundamental elements of the American political culture.

4. Compare and contrast the concepts of liberalism and conservatism.

ANSWERS TO THE PRACTICE EXAM

Fill-in-the-Blank

1. Conflict   [p. 7]
2. Authority   [p. 8]
3. Direct democracy   [p. 10]
4. Representative democracy   [p. 13]
5. Stability   [p. 15]
6. Groups   [p. 16]
7. Family   [p. 17]
8. Political culture   [p. 18]
9. Increased   [p. 22]
10. Liberalism, Conservatism   [p. 24]

True/False

1.	T	[p. 7]	3.	T	[p. 10]	5.	T	[p. 13]	7.	T	[p. 16]
2.	T	[p. 8]	4.	F	[p. 13]	6.	F	[p. 15]	8.	F	[p. 18]

9. F [p. 22]
10. T [p. 22]

Multiple Choice

1.	d	[p. 6]	6.	c	[p. 13]	11.	d	[p. 16]	16.	d	[p. 24]
2.	c	[p. 10]	7.	d	[p. 14]	12.	c	[p. 16]	17.	d	[p. 20]
3.	b	[p. 10]	8.	a	[p. 14]	13.	c	[p. 17]	18.	d	[p. 20]
4.	a	[p. 10]	9.	d	[p. 14]	14.	c	[p. 17]	19.	c	[p. 23]
5.	c	[p. 11]	10.	a	[p. 15]	15.	c	[p. 18]	20.	c	[p. 22]

Short Essay

An adequate short answer consists of several paragraphs that relate to concepts addressed by the question. Always demonstrate your knowledge of the ideas by giving examples. The following represent major ideas that should be included in the short essay answer.

1.   Explain the role of politics in an organized society. p. 6-10.

   • Definitions of politics-Harold Lasswell, and your author's
   • Government and power
   • Authority and Legitimacy

2.   Explain the origins of democracy and the different types of democracy. p. 10-14

   • Athenian model of direct democracy- Every citizen has a responsibility to participate through initiative, referendum and recall.
   • Representative democracy-a Republic in which the people vote for representatives to make laws and other decisions for the people.
   • Principles of western representative democracy-the emphasis on elected officials making all policy decisions.
   • Constitutional democracy-Limited government, that is the power of government is limited by a written document or constitution.

3.   Define the fundamental values of the American political culture. p. 18-20.

   • Liberty- The greatest freedom of individuals that is consistent with the freedom of other individuals in society. Freedom of speech, and freedom of religion are good examples.
   • Equality-A concept that all people are of equal worth. This concept is often debated as to its meaning. Does it mean equal political status or equal opportunity? Perhaps the Internet will provide persons with a forum in which all are equal
   • Property-can be seen as giving its owner political power and the liberty to do whatever he or she wants.
   • These are the three core values often linked with majority rule.

4.   Compare and contrast the concepts of liberalism and conservatism.

- Ideology-a set of ideas about the goal of politics p. 24-25.
    - Liberals
    - Positive government action to solve social problems
    - Advocates for civil rights
    - Advocates for social change

    - Conservatives
    - Faith in the private sector to solve most social problems
    - Advocates for individual action to protect rights
    - Advocates for a return to traditional values

Chapter 2
THE CONSTITUTION

CHAPTER SUMMARY

The story of the creation of the constitution is told in each generation and is the key to understanding American Government and Politics. [p. 33]

Initial Colonizing Efforts

The first British settlement in North American was Roanoke Island, which mysteriously disappeared. Recent research has indicated that a severe drought must have wiped out the colony. Jamestown, Virginia and Plymouth, Massachusetts, in 1607 and 1620, respectively, were the first successful settlements. Additional settlements followed in Massachusetts and Connecticut. [p. 33-35]. See the Milestones in Early U.S. Political History on p. 35.

British Restrictions and Colonial Grievances

The British government decided to tax the colonists to pay for the French and Indian War expenses. The Sugar Act in 1764 and Stamp Act in 1765 led to the Boston Tea Party, which caused the British Parliament to pass The Coercive or (Intolerable) Acts in 1774. p. [35-36]

The Colonial Response: The Continental Congresses

The colonists responded to the British by the **First Continental Congress** held in 1774, which issued a petition of grievances, and attempted to create committees to bring the colonists together. The **Second Continental Congress** met in 1775, and fighting had already occurred between the colonists and the British. The Second Congress established an army, with George Washington as commander in chief. p. 36.

Declaring Independence

In early 1776, the Second Continental Congress approved the **Resolution of Independence** to establish legitimacy, and to seek foreign military aid. The Second Congress assigned Thomas Jefferson the task of writing a formal declaration of independence. This **Declaration of Independence** was approved on July 4, 1776, and contained three major principles, based on the ideas of English political philosopher John Locke. These concepts were natural rights, consent of the governed, and the right to change the government. [p. 37-38]

The Rise of Republicanism

Colonists, who called themselves Republicans, were opposed to any strong central government. They were a powerful political force in the creation of strong state government in the 1776 to 1780 time period. [p. 38

The Articles of Confederation: Our First Form of Government

In 1781, the Articles of Confederation, a voluntary association of independent states, were created. See Figure 2-1 p. 39 and Table 2-1 p. 40 for information on powers of this form of government. The lack of taxing authority made the Articles, too weak a form of government to survive. Shay's Rebellion in 1786, spurred political leaders to take action to change the Articles. p. [39-41]

Drafting the Constitution

The Annapolis Convention was called in 1786 to discuss the weaknesses of the national. At this meeting, a call was sent out for all of the states to attend a general convention in Philadelphia in May 1787. 55 delegates from every state, except Rhode Island, attended the Philadelphia convention. The delegates were mostly nationalists, but included monarchists, democratic nationalists, non-democratic nationalists, and some strong state government advocates.

The debates, which began the first day, produced two major plans. The **Virginia Plan**, which proposed an entirely new national government, favoring big states, and the **New Jersey Plan**, which was an amendment to the Articles of Confederation. The "Great Compromise" brokered by the Connecticut delegation broke the deadlock between these two proposals. This compromise called for a **bicameral legislature** for a new form of national government. Slavery and other issues between the agrarian South and the mercantile North were resolved by other compromises, including the Three-Fifths Compromise. p. 44. The final agreement included **separation of powers**, sometimes known as the **Madisonian model**, a system of **checks and balances**, and an **electoral college** to elect the president. [p. 41-48]. See Figure 2-2, p. 47 for a view of the check and balance system.

The Final Document

Thirty-nine delegates approved the Constitution on September 17, 1787. The document established five fundamental principles; 1. Popular sovereignty, 2. A republican form of government, 3. Limited government, 4. Separation of powers, and 5. A federal system. [p. 48]

The Difficult Road to Ratification

The opposing forces in the battle for ratification were the **Federalists**, in favor of ratification, and the **Anti-Federalists**, who were opposed to ratifying the Constitution as it was drafted. Hamilton, Madison, and Jay, wrote the Federalists Papers, which were influential in the success of the ratification effort. p. 48.
In 1788, the ninth state, New Hampshire, ratified the Constitution, to formally establish it. See Table 2-2, p. 50 for the ratification vote in each of the states.

The Bill of Rights

Ratification of the Constitution was probably dependent on the Federalists promises of amendments to the Constitution to protect individual liberties. James Madison culled through state convention recommendations to produce what became, the Bill of Rights. One of the amendments proposed, was not ratified until 1992, when it became the 27th amendment to the constitution. The 10 amendments of the Bill of Rights was ratified in 1791. [p. 51-52]

Altering the Constitution: The Formal Amendment Process

Amending the constitution is a two-step process. The first step is proposing a new amendment. This can be done by either a two-thirds vote in both houses of Congress or by a national convention called by Congress at the request of two-thirds of the states. The second step in amending the constitution is to ratify the amendment. Ratification can be done by either a three-fourths vote of the state legislatures or by a three-fourths vote of state conventions called to ratify the amendment. See Figure 2-3 on p. 54.
Congress has considered more than 11,00 amendments, of which 33 have been submitted for ratification, and only 27 have been ratified. See Table 2-3 on p. 55. Since 1919, most proposed amendments have had a seven-year ratification limit, but the 27th amendment ratified in 1992, took 203 years.

Informal Methods of Constitutional Change

While there have few formal amendments to the constitution over the centuries, informal change has occurred on a more frequent basis. These informal changes have been by legislation passed by Congress under the commerce clause, and Article III, Section 1 of the constitution. The constitution has changed by the creation of executive agreements by Presidents to conduct foreign policy. The Supreme Court has claimed the power of judicial review in the case of Marbury v. Madison (1803). p. 57. Finally, through the usage in day-to-day government activities, interpretation, custom and tradition have influenced the meaning of the constitution. [p. 57-58]

The Constitution: Why Is It Important Today?

The U.S. constitution is the longest-lived written document, and most imitated in the world. We must not take our constitution for granted, because many nations, such as China and Iraq, claim that they are people's democracies. We must support the reality of the constitutional concepts, and insist that our government enforce those concepts. [p. 58]

KEY TERMS

anti-federalist p. 48
bicameral legislature p. 43
checks and balances p. 46
confederation p. 39
electoral college p. 47
executive agreement p. 59
Federalist p. 48
First Continental Congress p. 36
Great Compromise p. 44
judicial review p. 57

Madisonian model p. 46
natural rights p. 38
ratification p. 48
representative assembly p. 34
Second Continental Congress p. 36
separation of powers p. 46
state p. 39
supremacy doctrine p. 44
unicameral legislature p. 39

OTHER RESOURCES

A number of valuable supplements are available to students using the Schmidt, Shelley, and Bardes text. The full list of the supplements is in the preface to this study guide. Ask your instructor how to obtain these resources. One supplement is highlighted here, the INFOTRAC Online Library.

INFOTRAC EXERCISES

Log on to http://www.infotrac-college.com.
Enter your Pass code that came with your textbook.
You can access the article by typing the exact phrase below.

Frail Precedents
Three-Judge Panels
This article discusses the pro-First Amendment rights decisions by three-judge Court of Appeals judges, whose decisions are usually over-turned by the U.S. Supreme Court. Among the cases listed are top-less dancers, and performance artists claiming their nude bodies are freedom of speech.

Study Questions
1. What is your understanding of First Amendment Rights?
2. Do you believe artist expression is protected by the First Amendment?
3. Why do you think Court of Appeals decisions are often overturned by the Supreme Court?

Restraint Key Word in Constitutional Amendments
The premise of this article is that in the 105th Congress, nine new constitutional amendments were proposed.

Study Questions
1. What group is reccomending restraint in the proposing of new constitutional amendments?
2. What guidelines does this group propose?
3. Do you agree with this concept of restraint of constitutional amendments?

PRACTICE EXAM
(Answers appear at the end of this chapter.)

Fill-in-the-Blank.   Supply the missing word(s) or term to complete the sentence.

1.   The passage of the Coercive Acts by the British Parliament was in response to the _____.

2.   The rights of "life, liberty, and the pursuit of happiness" are referred to as _____.

3.   A voluntary association of independent states is referred to as _____.

4.   The plan of government that introduced the idea of a bicameral legislature was the _____.

5.   The agreement that resolved the differences between the large and small states over representation in the new government was the _____.

6.   Nowhere in the _____ are the word slavery or slaves used.

7.   _____ was the name given to those who favored the adoption of the new constitution.

8.   The _____ are considered by many to be the best example of political theorizing ever produced in the United States.

9.   The _____ was one of the two "lost" amendments of the twelve bill of rights amendments that originally went to the states in 1789.

10. The _____ is the only court specially created in the Constitution.

True/False.   Circle the appropriate letter to indicate if the statement is true or false.

T   F   1.   The Mayflower Compact embodied the idea of majority rule as a theory of government.

T   F   2.   Thomas Paine's pamphlet, Common Sense, popularized the idea of independence from Great Britain

T   F   3.   According to the Declaration of Independence, these United Colonies are, and of right ought to be free and independent states.

T   F   4.   The most fundamental weakness of the Articles of Confederation was the inability of the Congress to raise money for the militia.

T   F   5.   A majority of delegates to the Constitutional convention were in favor of a stronger central government.

T   F   6.   The Virginia plan called for each state to have equal representation in the new government.

T   F   7.   The Anti-federalists believed that the central government should be strengthened over the states, because the states were apt to abuse personal liberties.

T   F   8.   The delegates to the Constitution Convention represented a good cross-section of eighteenth-century American society.

T   F   9.   The only way to formally amend the Constitution is by a 4/5 vote of all of the state legislatures.

T   F   10. An informal way to amend the Constitution is by judicial review.

Multiple Choice. Circle the correct response.

1. The "lost colony" was
    a. Roanoke.
    b. Richmond.
    c. Jamestown.
    d. Portsmouth.

2. The last of the thirteen colonies to be established was
    a. Rhode Island.
    b. Connecticut.
    c. New Hampshire.
    d. Georgia.

3. The British government imposed taxes on the American colonies to pay for
    a. war with Spain.
    b. the costs of westward expansion of colonies.
    c. the costs of the French and Indian War.
    d. the costs of exploring India.

4. Thomas Paine's pamphlet, *Common Sense*
    a. called for a cessation of hostilities against the British.
    b. pointed out in "common sense" terms why America should break with Britain.
    c. was a propaganda tool used by the British to gain popular consent to their governing of the colonies
    d. apparently had very little effect on popular opinion about the revolution.

5. One of the revolutionary ideas of John Locke was the idea that people have
    a. a right to a secure job.
    b. a right to welfare if they need it.
    c. natural rights.
    d. a right to checks and balances in government.

6. During the Revolutionary War, the creation of state governments was strongly influenced by groups calling themselves
    a. Federalists.
    b. Democrats.
    c. Republicans.
    d. Monarchists.

7. The government under the Articles of Confederation Congress included a
    a. president, but no congress.
    b. congress and a president.
    c. unicameral legislature.
    d. strong central government.

8. Under the Articles of Confederation,
    a. each state had one vote.
    b. the national courts were the supreme authority.
    c. the congress imposed heavy taxes.
    d. the president ultimately controlled the government.

9. An important accomplishment of the Articles of Confederation was
    a. the creation of a common currency.
    b. settling states' claims to western lands.
    c. the creation of national tax collections.
    d. the creation of a strong national army.

10. Under the Article of Confederation, the Congress had the power to
    a. declare war and make peace.
    b. draft soldiers into military service.
    c. compel states to pay their share of national government costs.
    d. regulate interstate and foreign commerce.

11. Shay's rebellion demonstrated that the central government
    a. had the capability to protect citizens from riots and civil unrest.
    b. could not protect the citizenry from armed rebellion.
    c. dared not confront state militias.
    d. could easily incite citizens to riot.

12. The only state that refused to send delegates to the Constitution Convention was
    a. New Hampshire.
    b. Rhode Island.
    c. New York.
    d. Virginia.

13. The proceedings in the Constitutional Convention were kept secret because
    a. the delegates were doing something illegal.
    b. the public would not understand the issues involved and would create confusion.
    c. all meetings of this nature must be secret.
    d. if the proceeding were public, the delegates might have a more difficult time compromising on issues.

14. The Great Compromise
    a. resulted in the Bill of Rights being added to the Constitution.
    b. broke the deadlock between the large and small states over the nature of representation in the new national government.
    c. established the Electoral College as the vehicle for electing the president.
    d. allowed George Washington to be nominated and elected the first president.

15. The Madisonian Model of a government scheme refers to
    a. direct democracy.
    b. judicial review.
    c. a separation of powers.
    d. the supremacy of national laws over state laws.

16. The power of judicial review comes from
    a. the Constitution
    b. the Bill of Rights
    c. the case of *Marbury v. Madison*
    d. executive agreements

17. Which of the following are ways to amend the Constitution?
    a. a majority vote of citizens
    b. a majority vote of Congress
    c. a two-thirds vote of Congress
    d. judicial review by the Supreme Court

18. The Federalists Papers were
    a. largely written by Thomas Jefferson
    b. so brilliant, the Anti-Federalists could not respond
    c. not very significant as political theory
    d. responded to by Anti-Federalist political theory

19. The leading political figure responsible for recommending the Bill of Rights was
    a. Jefferson
    b. Madison
    c. Washington
    d. Franklin

20. Which of the following was not mentioned in the Constitution?
    a. the electoral college
    b. the Supreme Court
    c. political parties
    d. a national convention to propose constitutional amendments

Short Essay Questions. Briefly address the major concepts raised by the following questions.

1. Identify the milestone political documents that moved the colonies from the Mayflower Compact to the Constitutional Convention.

2. Trace the events and circumstances that led to the Revolutionary War.

3. Summarize the events leading to the call for a Constitutional Convention.

4. Explain the compromises over the organization of the government designed by the delegates to the Constitutional Convention.

ANSWERS TO THE PRACTICE EXAM

Fill-in-the-Blank.

1. Boston Tea Party   [p. 36]
2. Natural rights   [p. 38]
3. Confederation   [p. 39]
4. Virginia Plan   [p. 43]
5. Great Compromise   [p. 44]
6. Constitution   [p. 44]
7. Federalists   [p. 48]
8. Federalists Papers   [p. 49]
9. 27th Amendment   [p. 55]
10. Supreme Court   [p. 56]

True/False.

1.	T	[p. 35]	3.	F	[p. 37]	5.	T	[p. 43]	7.	F	[p. 49]	9.	F	[p. 54]
2.	T	[p. 36]	4.	T	[p. 40]	6.	F	[p. 43]	8.	F	[p. 49]	10.	T	[p. 57]

Multiple Choice.

1.	a	[p. 33]	6.	c	[p. 39]	11.	b	[p. 41]	16.	c	[p. 57]
2.	d	[p. 35]	7.	c	[p. 39]	12.	b	[p. 42]	17.	d	[p. 57]
3.	c	[p. 35]	8.	a	[p. 39]	13.	d	[p. 42]	18.	d	[p. 49]
4.	b	[p. 36]	9.	b	[p. 40]	14.	b	[p. 44]	19.	b	[p. 52]
5.	c	[p. 38]	10.	a	[p. 40]	15.	c	[p. 46]	20.	c	[p. 58]

Short Essay.

An adequate short answer consists of several paragraphs that relate to concepts addressed by the question. Always demonstrate your knowledge of the ideas by giving examples. The following represent major ideas that should be included in the short essay answer.

1. Identify the milestone political documents that moved the colonies from the Mayflower Compact to the Constitutional Convention. [p. 35-41]

    *   Refer to the time line on page 35 to give you a good overview of the question.
    *   The Mayflower Compact of 1620 was a political agreement derived from the consent of the people.
    *   The Fundamental Orders of Connecticut, 1639, was the first written constitution.
    *   The Massachusetts Body of Liberties, 1641, was the first constitution to include protection of individual rights.
    *   The Pennsylvania Charter of Privileges, 1701, contained a constitution and bill of rights and offered a precedent and rationale for our national Constitution.
    *   The Declaration of Independence, 1776, advocated independence from Great Britain.
    *   The Articles of Confederation, 1781, described the first attempt at an independent national government based on a confederation.

2. Trace the events and circumstances that led to the Revolutionary War. [35-39]

    *   Address this question in chronological/historical order.
    *   Explain the reasons for British restrictions represented by the Sugar Act, Stamp Act, and Coercive Act.
    *   Describe the colonial response as seen in the First and Second Continental Congresses, and Paine's *Common Sense*.
    *   Describe the Resolution of Independence and Declaration of Independence.

3. Summarize the events that lead to the call for the Constitutional Convention. [p. 39-41]

    *   Explain the development of the Articles of Confederation structure and the distribution of power.
    *   Explain the weaknesses of the Articles of Confederation as seen in the lack of good will among the states and the inability to tax for national needs.
    *   Explain the impact of Shay's Rebellion

17

4.   Explain the compromises that evolved at the Constitutional Convention and pertained to the organization of the government. [41-48]

- Discuss the various proposed structures for the new government as seen in the Virginia Plan and the New Jersey Plan
- Describe the Great Compromise.
- Discuss the distribution of governmental power as represented by Madison's theories of a separation of powers and a system of checks and balances.

Chapter 3
FEDERALISM

CHAPTER SUMMARY

Government in the United States consists of one national government, fifty state governments, and so many local governments to create a grand total of more than 80,000. See Table 3-1, p. 81.

Three systems of Government

There are basically three ways of organizing governmental structures. See figure 3-1 p. 83 for flow of power in the three systems. A Unitary system allows ultimate governmental authority in the national government. A Confederate system is a league of independent states. A Federal system divides government authority between a national government and state government [p. 81-82]

Why Federalism?

The United State developed a federal system because it was a practical solution, which retained state traditions and local power while it created a strong national government. Federalism also solved the problem of geographical size and regional isolation. Other arguments for federalism are it diffused political dissatisfaction among the different governments, provided a training ground for future national leaders, allowed diverse groups to develop in their own regions, and brought government closer to the people. p. 82-83 Certainly not every political viewpoint supported federalism. Some of the arguments against federalism are it provided a way for powerful state and local interests to block national progress, allowed for the possibility of expansion of national powers at the expense of states, and provided a way for powerful state and local interests to deny equal rights for minorities. [p. 84]

The Constitutional Basis for American Federalism

While the Constitution does not directly refer to federalism, it does divide government power into national government, state government, and powers prohibited to government. National government power can be described as enumerated, implied, and inherent. Enumerated powers are found in the first seventeen clauses of Article I, Section 8. Implied powers come from the necessary and proper clause, the last clause of Article I, Section 8. Inherent powers come from the fact that governments have an inherent right to ensure their own survival. Powers given to state governments called reserved powers, come from the 10th Amendment, which states that power not enumerated or denied, is reserved to the states. A major state power is police power, which is the authority to legislate for the health, morals, safety, and welfare of the citizens of the states. National and state government shares some powers, like the power to tax. These shared powers are called concurrent powers. p. 90. Powers denied to government are called prohibited powers, and deny powers to both national and state governments. The supremacy clause, Article VI, Paragraph 2 provided that federal laws are superior to all conflicting state and local laws. [p. 84-89]

Defining Constitution Powers-The Early Years

To be effective over the centuries, the constitution had to be vague and flexible. Two vague areas that were subject to the interpretation of the Supreme Court were the necessary and proper, and commerce clauses. In the case of **McCulloch v. Maryland (1819)**- p. 89 Chief Justice John Marshall ruled that the necessary and proper clause of Article I, Section 8 embraced ⌐all means, which are appropriate to carry out, the legitimate ends of the Constitution. In **Gibbons v. Ogden (1824)**-p. 91 Chief Justice Marshall ruled that the power to regulate interstate commerce in Article I, Section 8 was an exclusive national power.

States' Rights and the Resort to Civil War

The Jacksonian era (1829-1837) created a climate, in which most Southern states attempted to nullify national laws, and to justify secession from the federal union. The defeat of the South in the Civil War ended the theory of nullification and secession. The war effort created a larger and more powerful national government, which for the first time imposed an income tax on its citizens. [p. 91-92]

The Continuing Dispute over the Division of Power

Although the outcome of the Civil War established the supremacy of the national government, the debate over the division of authority continued through the stages of dual federalism, cooperative federalism, and new federalism. In dual federalism, which faded in the 1930's, the state governments and national government are viewed as separate entities, like separate layers in a cake. p. 93. Cooperative Federalism, which was created to deal with the disaster of the depression, advocated the state governments and national government should cooperate in solving problems, like merged layers in a marble cake. In the 1960's, another metaphor for cooperative federalism developed called Picket-fence Federalism. This added local government to the federal mix, and was explained as, the horizontal boards in the fence represent the national, state and local governments, while the vertical pickets represent different programs and policies in which each level of government works to the develop the policy represented by the picket. [p. 94]

Federal Grant-in-aid

The key factors in understanding how these different types of federalism developed were Federal grants-in-aid. The three major types of federal grants are categorical grants-in-aid designed for very specific programs or projects of state and local governments, matching funds, which require state and local governments to put up a share of the money, and equalization funds, which takes into account the relative wealth of the state or local entities. See Figure 3-2 for each government spending. p. 95. Block Grants were developed under the administration of Ronald Reagan in 1980. These grants are federal programs that provide funding to state and local government for general functional areas, with fewer restrictions than grants-in-aid. p. 96. One of the major barriers to returning authority to state government is federal mandates. A federal mandate is a requirement in federal legislation that forces states and local governments to comply with certain rules.

Federalism and the Supreme Court

President George W. Bush emphasized this concept of Federalism, when he said "the people" should decide public policy for themselves at the state and local level. The tragic events of September 11, 2001 have meant that, as President George W. Bush has had to make important decisions at the national level of public policy. However, in the 1990's, the Supreme Court sought to limit national government power under the 10th amendment, and the commerce clause. In the case of **United States v. Lopez** (1995)-the Gun-Free School Zones Act of 1990, based on Congress power under the commerce clause, was ruled unconstitutional. In **Printz v. United States** (1997) -provisions of the Brady Handgun violence Prevention Act of 1993, that required state employees to enforce these provisions, was ruled unconstitutional. [p. 97-99] See figure 3-3, p. 99 about differences in prison sentences in different states.

Federalism: Why Is It Important Today?

Our federal form of government means diversity because different state and local governments have different laws, and policies. This can create conflict between states, and between the state and national government. Some of these conflicts, which may be important to you, are discussed in these chapters. They include, educational standard, welfare payments, physician-assisted suicide, and the use of medical marijuana. [p. 99]

KEY TERMS

block grants- p. 96
categorical grant-in-aid- p. 95
commerce clause- p. 91
concurrent powers- p. 87
confederal system- p. 82
cooperative federalism- p. 94
dual federalism- p. 93

federal mandate p. 96
elastic clause- p. 86
enumerated powers- p. 85
police power- p. 86
supremacy clause- p. 87
unitary system- p. 81

INFOTRAC EXERCISES

Log on to http://www.infotrac-college.com.
Enter your Pass code that came with your textbook.
You can access the article by typing the exact phrase below.

States Immune Suit
Individuals Disabilities
Education Act
The premise of this article is that when a state accepts federal funding for education, the state must provide a free appropriate education for students with disabilities. Citizens can suit the state, if this is not done.

Study Questions
1. How does the Eleventh Amendment fit into this case?
2. What other case is cited, which establishes when a state has exceeded its constitutional authority?
3. Do you agree with the ruling in this case?

PRACTICE EXAM
(Answers appear at the end of this chapter.)

Fill-in-the-Blank.   Supply the missing word(s) or term to complete the sentence.

1. A system of government in which power is divided between a central, and subdivision governments is called a _____ system.

2. _____ powers are those that are derived from the fact that the United States is a sovereign power among the nations.

3. The Tenth Amendment establishes the _____ powers to the states.

4. The denial of power to state and national government referred to as _____
_____.

5. The legitimate exercise of national government power _____ any action by states.

6. The issue in the McCulloch v. Maryland case was whether the national government has _____ powers.

7. President Reagan and Congressional Republicans supported the development of_____ grants.

8. The doctrine that emphasizes a distinction between federal and state spheres of governmental authority is referred to as _____ _____.

9. A major set of block grants related to state _____ programs.

10. _____ _____ require state and local governments to comply with certain rules.

True/False - Circle the appropriate letter to indicate if the statement is true or false.

T   F   1. A unitary system of government is the easiest system to define.

T   F   2. The United States Constitution expressly designates that we should have a federal system of government.

T   F   3. The national government may deny the use of reserved powers to the states.

T   F   4. The Tenth Amendment provides for the reserved powers to the states.

T   F   5. Most concurrent powers of the states are specifically stated in the Constitution.

T   F   6. The Civil War permanently ended the idea that any state can claim the right to secede.

T   F   7. Chief Justice John Marshall was a strong supporter of state's rights.

T   F   8. The case of McCulloch v. Maryland (1819) set a precedent for a narrow interpretation of the implied powers of Congress.

T   F   9. Dual federalism emphasizes a distinction between federal and state spheres of authority.

T   F   10. There are great differences in prison sentences even between counties in the same state.

Multiple choice - Circle the correct response. The correct answers are at the end of the chapter.

1. The most popular way of ordering relations between central government and local units is by a
    a. Confederate system
    b. Federal system
    c. Unitary system
    d. Constitutional system

2. If ultimate governmental authority rests in the hands of a central government, that is a
    a. Federal system
    b. Confederate system
    c. Unitary system
    d. Theocratic system

3. A league of independent states, where the central government has only those matters expressly delegated to it, is a
    a. Federal system
    b. Confederate system
    c. Unitary system
    d. Democratic system

4.   To the framers of the Constitution, the appeal of federalism was that it
       a.   Allowed the states to control the process of government decision-making.
       b.   Retained state traditions and local power while it established a strong national government
       c.   Was acceptable to the British Parliament
       d.   Did not change the status quo

5.   The essential argument in *Federalist Paper No. 10* is that
       a.   A unitary government is the best kind of government for a diverse society
       b.   Smaller political units are likely to be dominated by a single political group
       c.   A unitary system of government is the most efficient
       d.   Only with a strong chief executive can the U.S. maintain its independence in world
       politics

6.   A special category of national powers that are not implied by the necessary and proper clause consists of
       those labeled as
       a.   inherent powers
       b.   enumerated powers
       c.   extraordinary powers
       d.   elongated powers

7.   The constitutional concept of police powers is created by the
       a.   10th Amendment
       b.   necessary and proper clause
       c.   interstate commerce clause
       d.   combined power clause

8.   The issue in McCulloch v. Maryland was
       a.   judiciary supremacy of the Supreme Court
       b.   the use of delegated power by the president
       c.   the commerce clause to regulate shipping on the open seas
       d.   the use of implied powers by the national government

9.   Grants to state and local governments designed for very specific programs and projects are referred to as
       a.   block grants
       b.   revenue sharing
       c.   unfunded mandates
       d.   categorical grants-in-aid

10.   Picket-fence federalism refers to
       a.   state and local governments
       b.   restoring more power to the national government
       c.   Congress
       d.   child labor laws

11.   Because of the supremacy clause the states cannot
       a.   deny citizens of another state the same privileges and immunities they extend to their own citizens
       b.   use their reserved or concurrent powers to thwart national policies
       c.   discriminate against citizens from another state.
       d.   Tax their citizens beyond national governmental rates

12. Picket-fence federalism added what element to the national and state governments.
    a. interest groups
    b. local government
    c. multi-national corporations
    d. political parties

13. In the cases of Printz v. U.S. and U.S. v. Lopez, the Supreme Court ruled that
    a. the national government exceeded its regulatory powers
    b. the state government exceeded its reserved powers
    c. the local government exceeded its police powers
    d. both state and national government exceeded constitutional powers

14. The concept of cooperative federalism was coined by political scientists after the administration of
    a. George Washington
    b. Abraham Lincoln
    c. Franklin D. Roosevelt
    d. Ronald Reagan

15. The case of United States v. Morrison dealt with the issue of
    a. Congress overreaching its authority
    b. states overreaching their authority
    c. private foundations overreaching their authority
    d. multi-national corporations overreaching their authority

16. Block grants are a tool, which helped establish
    a. less restrictions on state and local governments
    b. dual federalism
    c. more strings on state and local governments
    d. no difference in federalism

17. Federal Mandates are
    a. programs funded by Congress
    b. programs funded by states
    c. programs not required to be funded
    d. being phased out by Congress

18. Which Supreme Court case involved an issue of the Eleventh Amendment?
    a. Marbury v. Madison
    b. U.S. v. Lopez
    c. U.S. v. Morrison
    d. Alden v. Maine

19. The Violence against Women law was ruled
    a. constitutional in Kimel v. Florida
    b. constitutional in Alden v. Maine
    c. unconstitutional in U.S. v. Morrison
    d. unconstitutional in Printz v. U.S.

20. The diversity of our federal system means that citizens
    a. will get unfair prison sentences
    b. will get unequal welfare payments
    c. will get unequal educations funding
    d. will be able to "vote with their feet" to obtain policies they prefer

Short Essay Questions. Briefly address the major concepts raised by the following questions.

1. Discuss the three ways of organizing relations between a central government and local governmental units.

2. Identify and explain the division of powers between the national and state governments in the Constitution.

3. Trace and explain the debate over the division of powers between national and state government, since the Civil War.

4. Discuss the latest trends in our federal system, including federal mandates, Supreme Court decisions, and competitive federalism.

ANSWERS TO THE PRACTICE EXAM

Fill-in-the-Blank.

1. federal   [p. 82]
2. inherent   [p. 86]
3. reserved   [p. 86]
4. prohibited powers   [p. 87]
5. preempt   [p. 88]
6. implied   [p. 91]
7. block   [p. 96]
8. dual federalism   [p. 93]
9. welfare   [p. 96]
10. federal mandates   [p. 96]

True/False.

1.	T	[p. 81]	3.	F	[p. 86]	5.	F	[p. 87]	7.	F	[p. 92]	9.	T	[p. 93]
2.	F	[p. 84]	4.	T	[p. 86]	6.	T	[p. 92]	8.	F	[p. 91]	10.	T	[p. 99]

Multiple Choice.

1.	c	[p. 81]	6.	a	[p. 86]	11.	b	[p. 88]	16.	a	[p. 96]
2.	c	[p. 81]	7.	a	[p. 86]	12.	b	[p. 94]	17.	b	[p. 96]
3.	b	[p. 82]	8.	d	[p. 91]	13.	a	[p. 98]	18.	d	[p. 98]
4.	b	[p. 83]	9.	d	[p. 95]	14.	c	[p. 94]	19.	c	[p. 98]
5.	b	[p. 84]	10.	a	[p. 94]	15.	a	[p. 98]	20.	d	[p. 99]

Short Essay.

An adequate short answer consists of several paragraphs that relate to concepts addressed by the question. Always demonstrate your knowledge of the ideas by giving examples. The following represent major ideas that should be included in the short essay answer.

1. Discuss the three ways of organizing relations between a central government and local governmental units.

    - Refer to Figure 3-1 on page 83 for a view of the three ways and how power flows in each.
    - Unitary system in which a centralized government gives some powers to local or sub-divisional governments. p. 81.
    - Confederal system in which a league of independent states gives some power to the central Federal system in which power is divided between a central government p. 82.
    - Federal system in which power is divided between a central government and regional or sub-divisional governments. p. 82.

2. Identify and explain the division of powers between the national and state governments in the Constitution/

    - Expressed or enumerated powers are national government powers from Article 1, Section 8. p. 85
    - Implied powers are national government powers from the necessary and proper clause. p. 86
    - Concurrent powers are powers shared by national and state government. p. 87.
    - Reserved powers are state powers from the 10th amendment to the Constitution. p. 86.
    - Supremacy clause makes federal law supreme over conflicting state and local law. p. 87-88.

3. Trace and explain the debate over the division of powers between national and state government, since the Civil War.

    - Dual federalism is the system of government in which the states and national government each remain supreme within their own spheres. p. 93.
    - Cooperative federalism is the system in which the states and national government should cooperate in solving problems. Federal grants-in-aid are the main factor in developing cooperative federalism. P. 94-95.
    - Picket-fence Federalism involves state, and local government. p. 94.

4. Discuss the latest trends in our federal system, including federal mandates, and Supreme Court decisions.

    - Federal mandates are a requirement that forces states and local government to comply with certain rules, and are a major barrier to new federalism. p. 97
    - Printz v. U.S. case stuck down the provision of the Brady bill that required state employees to check the background of prospective handgun purchasers. p. 98
    - U.S. v. Lopez case held that the Gun-Free School Zones Act in 1990 exceeded Congress authority under the commerce clause of the constitution. p. 98
    - The Supreme Court rules that Congress has overstepped its authority under the commerce clause and 10th and 11th Amendments in the case of United States v. Morrison, Alden v. Maine, and Kimel v. Florida Board of Regents. p. 98

Chapter 4
CIVIL LIBERTIES

CHAPTER SUMMARY

Civil Liberties and the Fear of Government

Civil liberties refer to restraining the government's actions against individual rights outlined in the Bill of Rights. A few rights, like prohibiting ex post facto laws are found in Article I, Section 9 of the Constitution. p. 109.

Extending The Bill of Rights To State Governments

Most citizens are not aware that the Bills of Rights originally applied only to the national government. The 14th Amendment ratified in 1868 seemed to apply civil liberties guaranteed by the national constitution to the states. Incorporation theory holds that the protections of the Bill of Rights are applied to state governments by the 14th Amendment's due process clause. The Supreme Court has gradually and not completely accepted this theory. The first right to be incorporated was freedom of speech in Gitlow v. New York (1925). See Table 4-1 p. 110 for a list of cases incorporating various aspects of the Bill of Rights.

Freedom of Religion

The First Amendment to the Constitution begins with two basic principles of freedom of religion. The first is the no establishment clause, and the second is the free exercise of religion. The First Amendment begins with the words, "Congress shall make no law respecting an establishment of religion". The establishment clause or a "wall of separation of church and state", as Thomas Jefferson called it, covers such conflicts as state and local aid to religion, school prayer, and teaching of evolution versus creationism. In Lemon v. Kurtzman (1971) [p. 111], the Supreme Court ruled that direct state aid could not be used to subsidize religious instruction. This case created a three-part test for the no establishment clause. . In Agostini v. Felton (1997), the Court reversed itself, and ruled that federal funds for disadvantaged students attending religious schools did not violate the no establishment clause. [p. 112-113]. The use of public fund school vouchers for religious education has so far been upheld by the Supreme Court, but important issues remain. In the Engel v. Vitale case (1962) ruled that school sponsored prayer was a violation of the no establishment clause. The Wallace v. Jaffree (1985) struck down a minute of silent prayer in Alabama. Prayer outside the classroom was also limited in Lee v. Weisman (1992) in graduation ceremonies, and Santa Fe I.S.D. v. Doe for pre football game prayers. [p. 113-115]. The issue of teaching creationism was decided in the Edwards v. Aguillard case (1987), which ruled teaching the biblical story of creation was a violation of the no establishment clause. In recent years, the Supreme Court seemed to be lowering the barrier between church and state. In 1995, in Rosenberger v. University of Virginia, the Court ruled that the University must fund a Christian newsletter, if funding other campus group's newsletters. [p. 116-117]

The free exercise clause has usually focused on striking a balance between religious belief and religious practice. Religious practices can be regulated, as the case of Oregon v. Smith (1990), two Native-American drug counselors were fired for using peyote, an illegal drug, in their religious services. [p. 123]. In 1997, the Boerne. v. Flores case, ruled the Religious Freedom Restoration Act (RFRA) as unconstitutional for granting religious authorities too much power. [p. 117].

Freedom of Expression

Freedom of expression is probably the most used right that Americans have, but this right cannot be used to say anything at any time and any place. The Supreme Court has established some reasonable restrictions on free speech. The clear and present danger test from the **Schenck v. U.S.** case (1919) restricted speech, which provokes a "clear and present danger" to public order. The bad-tendency rule from **Gitlow v. N.Y.** (1925), limited speech that might lead to some evil. [p. 118] Prior restraint to regulate speech, which is censorship, has usually been ruled unconstitutional by the Court. Prior restraint also involves newspapers, movies, and TV shows. In one of the most famous cases, **New York Times v. U.S.** (1971), the Pentagon Papers case, the Supreme Court ruled the New York Times had the right to publish the information about the Vietnam War. [p. 119]. The Court has also given protection to symbolic and commercial speech, which involve the use of symbols to express opposition to the government, and free speech protection for advertising statements. In a highly controversial case, **Texas v. Johnson** (1989), flag burning was given protection as symbolic speech. [p. 120]. Clear areas of speech have not been considered constitutionally protected. These areas include obscenity, slander, fighting words, and hecklers' veto. The Supreme Court **in Miller v. California** (1973) created a four-part list of requirements for determining obscenity. Slander and libel are wrongfully injuring a person's reputation. Slander is spoken, and libel is written. Look for Court cases under freedom of the press. Fighting words, and hecklers' veto, are examples of individuals using their freedom of speech to deny rights to others. The Court has almost always ruled this type of speech unconstitutional. [p. 120-124].

Freedom of the Press

Freedom of the press can be viewed as printed speech, which means many concepts of freedom of expression apply to the press. Libel is the written defamation of a person's character. This is a major concern of mass media today. The Supreme Court in **New York Times v. Sullivan** (1964) gave some protection to media by ruling that public figures, which sue for libel, must prove actual malice on the part of the media. This greater burden of proof for public figures allows for the criticism of public officials and discussions of differences of opinion without fear of lawsuits. Another important issue for free press is the conflict between the public's right to know, and the rights of individuals or the police in the criminal justice system. In **Gannett Company v. De Pasquale** (1979), the Supreme Court ruled that a judge could issue a gag order to protect a defendant's right to a fair trial, from excessive news publicity. [p. 125]. The broadcast media, radio, TV, and movies, generally have more restrictions than print media because of the creation of the Federal Communication Commission regulations. The equal time rule, personal attack rule, and fairness doctrine, provide for broadcast media to all try to present both sides of an issue. [p. 125-126].

The Right to Assemble and to Petition the Government

This right often involves speech and press issues, since few demonstrations involve silent protests. The key issue is, how to balance this right, with the necessity for public officials to control traffic and maintain public order. The Supreme Court, in **Smith v. Collin** (1978), upheld the right of Nazis to march in the Chicago area, when they had been denied a parade permit by the city of Skokie, Illinois. [p. 126-127]

More Liberties under Scrutiny: Privacy Rights

The right to privacy has no explicit mention in the Constitution. It stems from the Supreme Court case, **Griswold v. Connecticut** (1965). The Court ruled that right to privacy stems from "penumbras" in the First, Third, Fourth, Fifth, and Ninth Amendments in the Bill of Rights. The information age, and the vast amount of information on the average citizen, has brought concern with privacy rights to the forefront of the public agenda. The first major application of privacy rights was **Roe v. Wade** (1973), in which the Supreme Court accepted the argument that laws against abortion violate a woman's right to privacy. [p. 128-130]. This decision has created, probably the most divisive public policy issue in America, even though later Court decisions placed restrictions on abortion rights. A second major application of right to privacy is the right to die. The New Jersey Supreme Court in the **Quinlan** case in 1976 established this principle. The U.S. Supreme Court modified this concept **in Cruzan v. Director, Missouri Department of Health** (1990). The Cruzan case has lead to the creation of "living wills" and other documents to provide safeguards to the right to die. In a related issue, the Court has left the right to assisted suicide to state government, which only Oregon allows. [p.132]. The September 11 attacks have produced an emphasis of security issues, which has lead to "roving" wiretaps.

The Great Balancing Act: The Rights of the Accused versus the Rights of Society

One of the most difficult areas of the constitution to balance the rights of individuals and the rights of society is in the rights of those accused of criminal offenses. The Fourth, Fifth, Sixth and Eight Amendments deal with the rights of criminal defendants. See a complete listing of these rights on [p. 133]. During the 1960's, the Supreme Court greatly expanded the rights of accused persons. In 1963, Gideon v. Wainwright granted a poor defendant, the right to an attorney, in most cases. In 1966, Miranda v. Arizona required police to inform an individual of their constitutional rights prior to questioning. Recent Court decisions have placed some restrictions on the Miranda ruling, in a continuing effort to find the right balance between individual, and societal rights. [p. 134]. The exclusionary rule, which prohibited the admission of illegally obtained evidence, during a trial, was applied to federal court in 1914. The concept was first applied to state courts in the case of Mapp v. Ohio (1961). Refer back to Table 4-1 [p. 110] for incorporation cases. Recent Court decisions have provided some discretion for police officers, who are acting in "good faith" [p. 136]. The Death Penalty is one of the most debated aspects of our criminal justice system because of the 8th Amendment protection against "cruel and unusual" punishment. In 1972, the Supreme Court ruled in Furman v. Georgia that the death penalty was random and arbitrary. This case was based on the existing state laws of the death penalty, which have been changed, and today exist in 38 states [p. 136]. See figure 4-1, p. 137. In 1996, Congress passed the Anti-Terrorism and Effective death Penalty Act. This sharply reduced the time for death-row appeals. [p. 138]. The growth of the Internet will produce new challenges in defining free expression rights. Hate speech is very difficult to deal with. The exercise of religious rights, particularly in institutions like schools, continues to stir controversy. The protection of privacy rights in our online culture, and the issues of abortion and the right to die continue to defy solutions. Crime will continue to be a problem as our society looks for new ways to balance the rights of the accused with the rights of us all [p. 137-138].

Civil Liberties: Why Are They Important Today?

In the past, every time there was a crisis, civil liberties were jeopardized. Today, we are in a time of crisis because of the war on terrorism, and civil liberties are threatened. We must not take our civil liberties for granted.

KEY TERMS

Actual malice - p. 126
Civil Liberties - p. 109
Clear and present danger - p. 118
Establishment clause - p. 111
Exclusionary rule - p. 135
Fighting words - p. 123
Free exercise clause - p. 117

Incorporation theory - p. 110
Libel - p. 124
Prior restraint - p. 119
Public figures - p. 125
Slander - p. 123
Symbolic speech - p. 119
Writ of *habeas corpus* - p. 132

INFOTRAC EXERCISES

Log on to http://www.infotrac-college.com.
Enter your Pass code that came with your textbook.
Use the CD that came with your textbook for suggestions for articles in this chapter.

PRACTICE EXAM

(Answers appear at the end of this chapter.)

Fill-in-the-Blank. Supply the missing word(s) or term to complete the sentence.

1. _____ _____ involve restraining the government's actions against individuals.

2. It was not until the _____ Amendment was ratified that our Constitution explicitly guaranteed due process of law to everyone.

3. The Lemon Test explains the concept of the _____ _____ in freedom of religion.

4. According to the _____ _____ rule, speech or other First Amendment freedoms may be curtailed if there is a possibility that such expression might lead to some evil.

5. The burning of the American flag as part of a peaceful protest is expressive conduct considered
   _____ _____.

6. For slander to be judged as defamation of character there must be a _____ _____ witness.

7. Only when a statement is made with_____ _____ can a public official receive damages for libel.

8. In the 1990s, the most controversial aspect of the right-to-die is _____ assisted suicide.

9. The _____, _____, _____, and _____ Amendments specially deal with the rights of criminal defendants.

10. The use of illegally seized evidence is prohibited in a trial because of the _____ rule.

True/False. Circle the appropriate letter to indicate if the statement is true or false.

T   F   1. The concept of civil liberties mainly refers to laws passed by Congress to limit government power.

T   F   2. As originally presented, the bill of Rights limited only the powers of the states, not the national government.

T   F   3. Most of the guarantees in the Bill of Rights now apply to the fifty states.

T   F   4. The use of state aid to private religious schools has generally been accepted by the Supreme Court.

T   F   5. For the most part, Americans are very limited in their ability to criticize public officials.

T   F   6. The federal courts have not extended constitutional protections of free speech, which is considered obscene.

T   F   7. Gag orders restrict the publication of news about a trial in progress or a pretrial hearing.

T   F   8. The right of privacy is explicitly guaranteed in the Bill of Rights.

T   F   9. The Webster and Planned Parenthood decisions have made it much easier to obtain a legal abortion.

T   F   10. The United States has one of the highest violent crime rates in the world.

Multiple Choice Circle the correct response.

1. When we are speaking of civil liberties, we are referring to limitations on government as outlined in the
   a. Declaration of Independence
   b. Magna Carta
   c. Articles of Confederation
   d. Bill of Rights

2. The view that most of the protections of the Bill of Rights are included under the fourteenth Amendment's protection against state government is called the
   a. inclusionary theory
   b. nullification theory
   c. necessary and proper theory
   d. incorporation theory

3. The three-part Lemon test concerns the issue of
    a. symbolic speech
    b. state aid to church-related schools
    c. presentation of evidence before a grand jury
    d. the right-to-die

4. The free exercise clause in the First Amendment does not prevent the government from curtailing religious practices that
    a. work against public policy and the public welfare
    b. infringe on citizen's sensitivities
    c. are defined by media as "cult" religions
    d. are a willful violation of the Pledge of Allegiance at public school

5. According to the "clear and present danger" test
    a. a speech must be unclear as to its intent for it to be ruled unconstitutional.
    b. the action called for must be constitutionally "vague" in order to be ruled unconstitutional.
    c. free speech can be curbed if such speech would cause a condition that Congress has the power to prevent.
    d. Free speech may not be curbed, because speech alone cannot bring about action.

6. The burning of an American flag in a peaceful protest is an example of
    a. a violation of the Constitution
    b. a protected action under the clear and present danger concept
    c. a protected action under the symbolic speech concept
    d. an issue not yet decided by the Supreme Court

7. Paid advertising can be constitutionally protected as a form of
    a. commercial speech
    b. symbolic speech
    c. exempted speech
    d. private speech

8. The Miller v. California case created a list of requirements that apply to
    a. abortion
    b. religious freedom
    c. obscenity
    d. libel

9. Individuals using "fighting words" or exercising a "heckler's veto"
    a. are exercising constitutionally protected forms of speech
    b. are exercising constitutionally protected forms of freedom of religion
    c. are not within the bounds of constitutional protection
    d. are in a vague area that the federal courts have not ruled on

10. Public officials may sue for libel if they can prove the statement
    a. was false
    b. hurt the official's reputation
    c. hurt the official's feelings
    d. was made with actual malice

11. Gag orders are
    a. designed to eliminate illegal speech
    b. designed to eliminate unlawful assembly
    c. restrictions on the publication of news concerning pretrial hearing or trials in progress
    d. part of the controversy over the death penalty

12. The Roe v. Wade case decided the abortion issue on the basis of
    a. freedom of religion
    b. freedom of speech
    c. right to privacy
    d. the incorporation concept

13. The Exclusionary rule prohibits
    a. defendants from testifying in their own behalf
    b. improperly obtained evidence from being used by prosecutors
    c. a spouse from testifying in a criminal case
    d. the defense counsel form having access to the prosecution's evidence

14. The Exclusionary rule was first extended to state court proceedings in the Supreme Court case of
    a. Nix v. Williams
    b. Miranda v. Arizona
    c. Mapp v. Ohio
    d. Betts v. Brady

15. A technically incorrect search warrant can be legal under the concept of
    a. the Miranda rule
    b. the "good faith" exception
    c. the unreasonable search and seizure
    d. the right to an attorney if you cannot one

16. The case that ruled against the right to commit suicide was
    a. Cruzan v. Director, Missouri Dept. of Health
    b. Furman v. Georgia
    c. Washington v. Glucksberg
    d. Miranda v. Arizona

17. The Anti-Terrorism and Effective Death Penalty Act provided for
    a. immediate execution after the guilty verdict
    b. execution within a month after the guilty verdict
    c. a severe time limit on death-row appeals
    d. so called "three strikes" and you are out procedure

18. According to the text, a growing concern about free speech on the Internet is
    a. slander
    b. obscenity
    c. hate speech
    d. fraud in commercial speech

19. In the case of Doe v. University of Michigan (1989), the Court ruled the campus speech code was
    a. not covered by the U.S. Constitution
    b. constitutional
    c. constitutional with equal time for both sides
    d. unconstitutional

20. The Supreme Court in 2000 ruled that "partial-birth" abortions are
    a. unconstitutional
    b. not covered by Roe v. Wade
    c. constitutional
    d. constitutional, only if passed by state legislatures

Short Essay Questions   Briefly address the major concepts raised by the following questions.

1. Explain the historical context for the importance of the Bill of Rights within the Constitution.

2. Identify and explain the two concepts of freedom of religion contained in the First Amendment.

3. Discuss the important principles established by the Supreme Court for freedom of speech and press.

4. Outline and discuss the right of an individual accused of a crime.

ANSWERS TO THE PRACTICE EXAM

Fill-in-the-blank

1.	Civil Liberties	[p. 109]
2.	Fourteenth	[p. 110]
3.	establishment	[p. 111]
4.	bad-tendency	[p. 118]
5.	symbolic	[p. 120]
6.	third party	[p. 123]
7.	actual malice	[p. 125]
8.	physician	[p. 130]
9.	Fourth, Fifth, Sixth, Eighth	[p. 132]
10.	exclusionary	[p. 136]

True/False

1.	F	[p. 109]	3.	T	[p. 110]	5.	F	[p. 118]	7.	T	[p. 125]	9.	F	[p. 129]
2.	T	[p. 109]	4.	F	[p. 113]	6.	T	[p. 120]	8.	F	[p. 127]	10.	T	[p. 131]

Multiple Choice.

1.	d	[p. 109]	6.	c	[p. 120]	11.	c	[p. 125]	16.	c	[p. 131]
2.	d	[p. 110]	7.	a	[p. 120]	12.	c	[p. 128]	17.	c	[p. 138]
3.	b	[p. 111]	8.	c	[p. 121]	13.	b	[p. 136]	18.	c	[p. 124]
4.	a	[p. 117]	9.	c	[p. 123]	14.	c	[p. 136]	19.	d	[p. 124]
5.	c	[p. 118]	10.	d	[p. 125]	15.	b	[p. 136]	20.	c	[p. 130]

Short Essay.

An adequate short answer consists of several paragraphs that relate to concepts addressed by the question. Always demonstrate your knowledge of the ideas by giving examples. The following represent major ideas that should be included in the short essay answer.

1. Explain the historical context for the importance of the Bill of Rights within the Constitution.

    *   Few specific restrictions on government were contained in the constitution p. 109-110.
    *   The Bill of Rights did not apply to state governments.
    *   The Fourteenth Amendment guaranteed civil liberties of the Constitution applied to the states, which is called incorporation.
    *   Only gradually on a case-by-case basis, but never completely has the Supreme Court accepted incorporation.
    *   See Table 4-1 for a list of cases incorporating different constitutional rights

2. Identify and explain the two concepts of freedom of religion contained in the First Amendment.
    *   The establishment clause prohibits official government support of religion. p. 110-117.
        *   Lemon v. Kurtzman (1971) creates a three-part test of this concept.
        *   Engle v. Vitale (1962) ruled that official prayer in public school is unconstitutional.
        *   Teaching of evolution cannot be banned, and bible story of creation cannot be taught.
    *   The free exercise of religion shall not be prohibited. p. 119-120
        *   Religious beliefs are absolute, but religious practices, which work against public policy and public welfare may be restricted.
        *   Oregon v. Smith (1990) ruled that Native Americans could be deny unemployment benefits, when fired from a state job for using peyote in their religious services.
        *   Congress passed the Religious Freedom Restoration Act (RFRA) in 1993 to require all levels of government to "accommodate religious conduct".
        *   City of Boerne v. Flores (1997) ruled the RFRA law unconstitutional.

3. Discuss the important principles established by the Supreme Court for freedom of speech and press.

    *   Freedom of speech has never been considered absolute, so some restrictions are permitted p. 117-126.
        *   Schenck v. U.S. (1919), ruled on speech that provokes a "clear and present anger" that Congress has a right to prevent is not constitutionally protected.
        *   Gitlow v. New York (1925), held that expression that might lead to some "evil" is not protected.
        *   However, in the New York Times v. U.S. (1971), ruled that prior restraint or censorship is unconstitutional.
    *   Symbolic speech and commercial speech have received constitutional protection.
        *   Texas v. Johnson (1989), ruled that the burning of an American flag in a peaceful protest is protected as symbolic speech.
    *   Some speech has never been constitutionally protected.
        *   Miller v. California (1973), established a formal list of requirements for obscenity, which is not protected.
        *   Slander, the public uttering of a false statement that harms a person's reputation, is not protected.
        *   Fighting words, and heckler's veto are examples of using speech to prevent others from exercising their rights, and are not protected.
    *   Freedom of the press can be viewed as printed speech, so many of the same concepts apply. P. 126-128
        *   Libel is the written defamation of a person's reputation, but the press has some limited protect from libel.
        *   The New York Times v. Sullivan (1964), created the concept of a public figure, who must prove actual malice on the part of media, to be able to sue for libel.

- Another significant free press issue is conflict between free press and a criminal suspect's right to a fair trial. Gannett Company v. De Pasquale (1979), provided for judges to issue gag order to restrict the publication of news about pretrial hearings, or trials in progress.
- Broadcast media has generally not been protected like published materials. The federal Communication Commission (FCC) has created guidelines such as the equal time rule, personal attack rule, and the fairness doctrine.

4. Outline and discuss the right of an individual accused of a crime. p. 131-138.

- In the Bill of Rights, the 4th, 5th, 6th, and 8th Amendments deal with rights of criminal defendants. The process is divided into three parts.
    1. Limits on the conduct of police officers and prosecutors
    2. Defendant's pretrial rights
    3. Trial rights
- The 4th Amendment protects against an unreasonable search and seizure of evidence.
- The exclusionary rule prevents this evidence from being admitted at trial. Mapp v. Ohio extended the exclusionary rule to state courts.
- The 5th Amendment provides for the right to remain silent, to be informed of the charges, and the right to legal counsel. Miranda v. Arizona dealt with the right to be informed of your rights.
- The 6th Amendment provides for legal counsel during a trial, even if the defendant cannot one. Betts v. Brady applied this to capital cases. Gideon v. Wainwright applied this to felony offenses.

Chapter 5
CIVIL RIGHTS: EQUAL PROTECTION

CHAPTER SUMMARY

Civil Rights are the rights of all Americans to equal treatment under law, as provided in the Fourteenth Amendment to the Constitution. Essentially, the history of civil rights in America is the struggle of various groups to be free from discriminatory treatment. [p. 147].

African Americans and the Consequences of Slavery in the United States

Before 1863, the Constitution protected slavery. In *Dred Scott v. Sanford* (1857), the Supreme Court had upheld the constitutionality of slavery by ruling that slaves were not citizens of the United States [p. 147]. President Lincoln's Emancipation Proclamation in 1863, and the passage of the 13th, 14th, and 15th Amendments to the Constitution ended constitutional inequality. From 1865-1875, to protect African-American rights from being violated by state government, the Republican-controlled Congress passed several Civil Rights Acts [p. 148]. The Supreme Court ruled these acts unconstitutional, so they were largely ineffective. The most significant of these decisions was *Plessy v. Ferguson* (1896), which created the doctrine of separate-but-equal and led to racial segregation, particularly in the South. When federal troops that occupied the South were withdrawn in 1877, the Southern states restricted African-Americans' right to vote by imposing a number of laws, such as, the grandfather clause, poll taxes, and literacy tests. The white primary law was finally ruled unconstitutional in the 1944 case of *Smith v. Allwright*.[p. 150].

The end to the separate-but-equal doctrine, and racial segregation began in the 1930s with a series of lawsuits to admit African Americans to graduate and professional schools. These lawsuits culminated in the unanimous Supreme Court decision in *Brown v. Board of Education of Topeka* in 1954, which ruled that public school segregation of the races violates the equal protection clause of the 14th Amendment [p. 151]. In reaction to this decision, state governments sought loopholes in the decision and society witnessed a tremendous increase in private, often religion-based schools. The early attempts to integrate schools often relied on court-ordered busing of students across neighborhoods. Recently, the federal courts have returned authority to local school officials, as in *Missouri v. Jenkins* (1995), which allowed Missouri to stop financing a magnet school for racial integration [p. 152-154].

The Civil Rights Movement

The *Brown* decision was a moral victory, but did little to change the underlying structure of segregation. In 1955, an African-American woman, Rosa Parks, refused to give up her seat on the bus to a white man. She was arrested and fined. Thus began the civil rights protests that would eventually end racial segregation. Martin Luther King, Jr., a Baptist minister, organized a yearlong boycott of the Montgomery; Alabama bus line, the success of which propelled King to national leadership of the civil rights movement. The culmination of the movement came in 1963, when intending to influence Civil rights legislation then pending in Congress, Dr. King led a march on Washington D.C. and gave his famous "I have a dream" speech [p. 155-156].

Modern Civil Rights Legislation

In passing the Civil Rights Act of 1964, Congress had created the most far-reaching bill on civil rights in modern times. The Act demolished discrimination in all areas, except housing, which was covered in the Civil Rights Act of 1968. See p. 157 for the major provisions of the Act. Congress followed up the 1964 Act with the Voting Rights Act of 1965, which eliminated discriminatory voter-registration laws and authorized federal officials to register voters, primarily in the South. Subsequent amendments to the Voting Rights Act granted protections, such as bilingual ballots, to other minorities [p. 158]. Although there is increased voting participation among all minorities, there are lingering social and economic disparities. [p. 160]

Immigration and the Civil Rights Agenda

The concept of the melting pot in American society described the idea that immigrants could best succeed by adopting the language and political values of the dominant culture. Questioning the validity of this concept, many people today think that American society should be seen as a multicultural country. The lines separating racial groups are increasingly blurred. Golf professional Tiger Woods is an excellent example of this trend. [p. 162-163].

Women's Struggle for Equal Rights

Women first became involved politically in the abolition of slavery movement. From this effort, Lucretia Mott and Elizabeth Cady Stanton organized the first women's rights convention in 1848 [p. 163]. The 1870 campaign to ratify the 15th Amendment, which gave voting rights to African-American men, split the women's suffrage movement. But women successfully campaigned for passage of the 19th Amendment, which enfranchised women and was ratified in 1920 [p. 164].

[See Table 5-1 p. 164 for the year that women gained the right to vote in other countries]. After achieving the right to vote, women engaged in little political activity until the 1960s, when the feminist movement called for political, economic, and social equality for women. The feminist movement attempted to obtain the ratification of an Equal Rights Amendment in the 1970s, but the necessary 38 states failed to ratify [p. 165]. After this defeat, the women's movement began to work for women's increased representation in government. Political Action Committees, PACs, were created to fund women candidates. The largest of these PACs is EMILY's list, which stands for "Early Money Is Like Yeast—It Makes the Dough Rise" [p. 166]. Although no major political party has nominated a woman for president, women have run for the vice-presidency and serve as members of the cabinet and the Supreme Court. Women have been elected governors of major states; mayors of large cities, and about 22% are state legislators. In 2002, a woman was elected to a leadership post in Congress. Nancy Pelosi (D) California was elected Democrats minority whip in the U.S. House of Representatives. [p. 167]

Gender-Based Discrimination in the Workplace

Title VII of the Civil Rights Act of 1964 prohibited gender discrimination in employment, including sexual harassment. In 1991, it became apparent that these laws were not being vigorously enforced when Anita Hill charged Supreme Court nominee Clarence Thomas with sexual harassment. This publicity resulted in an increasing number of court cases dealing with sexual harassment. Supreme Court cases like *Faragher v. City of Boca Raton* (1998), and *Burlington Industries v. Ellerth* (1998), ruled that employers and employees were libel for sexual harassment if they did not exercise reasonable care to prevent and correct promptly any sexually harassing behavior [p. 168-169]. Another important issue for women in the workplace has been wage discrimination. Although the Equal Pay Act of 1963 was designed to provide for equal pay, a woman earns about seventy-eight cents for every dollar earned by a man. Some of the key reasons for this are the low pay for jobs traditionally held by women (such as child care), and the corporate "glass ceiling" that prevents women from reaching the highest executive positions in business [p. 169-170].

Civil Rights: Why Are They Important Today?

While African Americans, minorities, and women have made major gains since 1950, they remain under-represented in national politics and participation. The debate over the melting pot of cultures versus ethnic separatism or multiculturalism will continue. The role of women in the workplace and equal pay issues will continue to be a focus of national domestic policy [p. 170].

KEY TERMS

busing—p. 152
civil rights—p. 147
de facto segregation—p. 152
de jure segregation—p. 152
feminism—p. 165
gender discrimination—p. 165
Grandfather Clause—p. 151

literacy test—p. 151
poll tax—p. 151
separate-but-equal—p. 150
sexual harassment—p. 169
suffrage—p. 164
white primary—p. 150

INFOTRAC EXERCISES

Log on to http://www.infotrac-college.com.
Enter your Pass code that came with your textbook.
You can access the article by typing the exact phrase below.

Boston Board Abandons School Busing

The premise of this article is that the Boston School Board voting to end programs of assigning students to schools on the basis of race.

Study Questions
1. Why did the Boston School Board vote to end the desegregation practice of busing?
2. How do you feel about this decision?

PRACTICE EXAM
(Answers appear at the end of this chapter.)

Fill-in-the-Blank. Supply the missing word(s) or term(s) to complete the sentence.

1. In _____ v. _____, the Supreme Court confirmed the constitutionality of slavery

2. The constitutional principle that permitted racial segregation was called the _____ _____ _____ _____.

3. The obvious solution to both de facto and de jure segregation of schools was _____.

4. Martin Luther King Jr. philosophy of _____ included such tactics as demonstrations and marches.

5. The _____ _____ _____ of 1964 was the most far-reaching civil rights bill in modern times.

6. The _____ _____ _____ of 1965 outlawed discriminatory voter-registration tests.

7. The government faces the challenge today that lines separating racial groups are becoming increasingly _____.

8. By the year 2010, _____ will be the largest minority group in the United States.

9. The largest Political Action Committee for women candidates is called _____ list.

10. Barriers faced by women in the corporate world are referred to as the _____ _____.

True/False. Circle the appropriate letter to indicate if the statement is true or false.

T   F   1. The case of *Plessy v. Ferguson* created the separate-but-equal doctrine.

T   F   2. The Reconstruction statutes after the Civil War helped to secure civil rights for African-Americans equal to those of whites.

T   F   3.   Concentrations of minorities in defined geographic locations results in *de facto* segregation.

T   F   4.   The era of civil rights protests in the mid 1950s began with the boycott of public bus transportation in Montgomery, Alabama.

T   F   5.   The white primary was used in southern states to deny African-Americans the right to vote.

T   F   6.   African-Americans increased their political participation as a direct result of the Civil Rights Act of 1964.

T   F   7.   In the 2000 census, individuals were allowed to check more than one racial box.

T   F   8.   During the national debate over the ratification of the ERA, a women's countermovement to feminism emerged.

T   F   9.   No woman has ever held a leadership position in Congress.

T   F   10. Gender discrimination was prohibited by the Civil Rights Act of 1964.

Multiple-Choice. Circle the correct response.

1. The *Dred Scott* case
    a. freed the slaves in the South.
    b. contributed to a more peaceful resolution of the slavery issue.
    c. contributed to making the Civil War inevitable.
    d. provided full and equal citizenship for all African Americans.

2. The reconstruction statutes had the effect of
    a. securing equality for African Americans in their civil rights.
    b. doing little to secure equality for African Americans in their civil rights.
    c. restructuring society to provide for greater equality of opportunity.
    d. setting the stage for the Civil War.

3. The effect of *Plessy v. Ferguson* on racial segregation was to establish a
    a. "clear and present danger" principle to further integration.
    b. pattern to outlaw segregation in the South.
    c. pattern for racial integration throughout the country.
    d. constitutional cornerstone of racial discrimination throughout the country.

4. An unintended effect of the Supreme Court's direction of "all deliberate speed" toward achieving integation in public education was that it
    a. allowed some jurisdictions to integrate too quickly thereby causing confusion.
    b. provided the pattern for complete integration of public education.
    c. was used as a loophole by some jurisdictions to stall efforts toward integration.
    d. created an influx of rural students attending urban schools.

5. *De facto* segregation of school districts can come about through
    a. residential concentration of minorities in defined geographical locations.
    b. school boards drawing boundary lines to include only certain minority groups.
    c. Supreme Court edicts.
    d. a program of forced busing across district lines.

6. Recent Supreme Court decisions on busing to integrate public schools have emphasized
    a. more busing to fully integrate schools.
    b. spending more money to attract minority students without busing.
    c. stronger court controls over local schools.
    d. restoring more control to local schools.

7. Discrimination in most housing was forbidden by the
    a. Civil Rights Act of 1964.
    b. Civil Rights Act of 1968.
    c. Voting Rights Act of 1965.
    d. Equal Housing Act of 1965.

8. The first African American candidate to compete seriously for the presidential nomination was
    a. Jesse Jackson
    b. Clarence Thomas
    c. Thurgood Marshall
    d. Colin Powell

9. In terms of the women's movement in the U.S., the anti-slavery movement had the effect of
    a. retarding organized political action by women.
    b. enslaving women and creating a secondary status for them.
    c. creating the first political cause in which women could become actively engaged.
    d. allowing women to become the dominant force in this movement.

10. The vast majority of immigrants to the U.S. are from
    a. Eastern Europe
    b. The former Soviet Union
    c. Latin America
    d. The Middle East

11. The first woman appointed to a president's cabinet was
    a. Sandra Day O'Connor.
    b. Susan B. Anthony.
    c. Francis Perkins.
    d. Jeannette Rankin.

12. Today, the overall national turnout of women voters is
    a. higher than that of male voters.
    b. much less because politics is considered to be a male activity.
    c. slightly less than that of male voters.
    d. about the same as elderly voters.

13. Sexual harassment of women in the workplace is
    a. no longer prohibited by statute.
    b. prohibited by Title VII of the Civil Rights Act of 1964.
    c. considered "protective" legislation which the Supreme Court has ruled unconstitutional.
    d. considered a form of reverse discrimination against men.

14. The Equal Pay Act of 1963 has
    a.   never been enforced.
    b.   only applied when women and men do exactly the same job.
    c.   only applied to comparable worth situations.
    d.   totally equalized pay between women and men.

15. The issue of wage discrimination was first addressed
    a.   During the Civil War
    b.   During World War I.
    c.   During World War II
    d.   During the 1960's

16. The "glass ceiling" refers to
    a.   subtle barriers that prevent women from being promoted to top positions in corporations.
    b.   corporate espionage.
    c.   reverse discrimination against men.
    d.   national laws designed to protect women from wage discrimination.

17. Which President appointed the most women to his cabinet?
    a.   George W. Bush
    b.   Bill Clinton
    c.   Richard Nixon
    d.   George H. Bush

18. Which Supreme Court case ruled that Title VII protection applied to harassment by members of the same sex?
    a.   Oncale v. Sundowner Offshore Services, Inc.
    b.   Harris v. Forklift Systems, Inc.
    c.   Faragher v. City of Boca Raton
    d.   Burlington Industries v. Ellerth

19. In 2010, which group will constitute a majority of U.S. workers?
    a.   men
    b.   non citizens
    c.   people 65 years and older
    d.   women

20. Which of the following is a reason for a new civil rights agenda in the U.S.?
    a.   people have too many rights today.
    b.   discrimination has just about ended.
    c.   the old concepts of majority versus minority are no longer applicable.
    d.   War on Terrorism must create inequality.

Short Essay Questions. Briefly address the major concepts raised by the following questions.

1. Explain the impact on education of the Supreme Court's decision in *Brown v. Board of Education of Topeka*, and discuss what new problems the decision fostered.

2. Discuss the key events in the Civil Rights Movement that led to passage of the 1964 Civil Rights Act.

3. Discuss the provisions of the Voting Rights Act of 1965. What impact has this had on political participation among minority voters in the United States?

4. Explain the major issues of gender discrimination in the workplace.

ANSWERS TO THE PRACTICE EXAM

Fill-in-the-Blank.

1.	Dred Scott v. Sanford	[p. 147]
2.	separate-but-equal doctrine	[p. 150]
3.	busing	[p. 152]
4.	nonviolence	[p. 155]
5.	Civil Rights Act	[p. 157]
6.	Voting Rights Act	[p. 159]
7.	blurred	[p. 162]
8.	Hispanics	[p. 162]
9.	Emily's	[p. 166]
10.	glass ceiling	[p. 170]

True/False.

1.	T	[p. 150]	3.	T	[p. 152]	5.	T	[p. 150]	7.	T	[p. 163]	9.	F	[p. 167]
2.	F	[p. 149]	4.	T	[p. 154]	6.	F	[p. 158]	8.	T	[p. 165]	10.	T	[p. 168]

Multiple Choice.

1.	c	[p. 147]	5.	a	[p. 152]	9.	c	[p. 163]	13.	b	[p. 169]	17.	b	[p. 167]
2.	b	[p. 149]	6.	d	[p. 153]	10.	c	[p. 162]	14.	b	[p. 170]	18.	a	[p. 169]
3.	d	[p. 150]	7.	b	[p. 158]	11.	c	[p. 167]	15.	c	[p. 170]	19.	d	[p. 169]
4.	c	[p. 151]	8.	a	[p. 159]	12.	a	[p. 168]	16.	a	[p. 170]	20.	c	[p. 172]

Short Essay Answers

An adequate short answer consists of several paragraphs that relate to concepts raised by the question. Always demonstrate your knowledge of the ideas by giving examples. The following represent major ideas that should be included in these short essays.

1. Explain the impact on education of the Supreme Court's decision in *Brown v. Board of Education of Topeka* and discuss what new problems the decision fostered [p. 1516-152].

    *   The concept of separate-but-equal from *Plessy v. Ferguson* was overturned.
    *   The order to implement "with all deliberate speed" was used as a loophole by state officials to slow the pace of integration of schools.
    *   School integration in Little Rock, Arkansas, was blocked by use of the state's National Guard.
    *   President Eisenhower federalized the Arkansas National guard and integrated schools in Little Rock.
    *   *De Jure* segregation is illegal under the Brown decision.
    *   *De Facto* segregation because of housing patterns is dealt with by busing to achieve integration.

2. Discuss the key events in the Civil Rights Movement that led to the passage of the 1964 Civil Rights Act [p. 154-157].

    *   Rosa Parks refuses to move to the back of the bus, the "colored" section in Montgomery, Alabama.
    *   Martin Luther King, Jr leads a year-long African-American boycott of the Montgomery bus line.
    *   The Southern Christian Leadership Conference is formed.
    *   A series of nonviolent sit-ins, protests, demonstrations, and marches are held.
    *   Dr. King is arrested in Birmingham, Alabama, during a protest in which police use dogs and cattle prods on the demonstrators.
    *   Media coverage of these events has a profound effect on public opinion.
    *   Dr. King organizes a march on Washington, D.C., and delivers his famous "I have a Dream" speech, which is televised to millions.

3. Discuss the provisions of the Voting Rights Act of 1965. How did this law influence the political participation of minority voters in the United States [p. 158-160]?

    *   Provision One outlawed the discriminatory voter-registration test.
    *   Provision Two authorized federal registration of voters and federally administered voting procedures.
    *   African-American registration and voting increased dramatically.
    *   More African Americans became prominent in national politics.
    *   Hispanic registration and voting increased dramatically.
    *   Bilingual ballots were authorized.

4. Explain the major issues of gender discrimination in the workplace. [p. 168-170]

    *   Title VII of the Civil Rights Act of 1964 prohibits gender discrimination in the workplace.
    *   One major issue is sexual harassment. Sexual harassment has been extended to the employer who does nothing to stop sexual harassment by and employee through court decisions in *Faragher v. City of Boca Raton* (1998), and *Burlington Industries v. Ellerth* (1998).
    *   Second major issue is wage discrimination. The Equal Pay Act of 1963 prohibits unequal pay for men and women doing the same job. Comparable worth is the concept that takes into account skill, effort, and responsibility to determine pay, because traditional "women's" jobs pay less than traditional "men's" jobs. Women have a harder time getting high corporate positions because of the "glass ceiling".

Chapter 6
CIVIL RIGHTS: BEYOND EQUAL PROTECTION

CHAPTER SUMMARY

Minority groups and women granted equality by the Civil Rights Act of 1964, sometimes lacked the education and skills, because of past discrimination, to compete for educational admissions and jobs. [p. 179]

Affirmative Action

The government responding to remedy this situation created Affirmative Action in 1965. Affirmative Action is a policy to give special consideration to traditionally disadvantaged groups in an effort to overcome present effect of past discrimination. This policy ran into serious problems in 1978 in the Supreme Court case of **Regents of the University of California v. Bakke**, which involved admission policies at UC-Davis Medical School. Alan Bakke argued that the affirmative action admission policy requiring a racial quota was reverse discrimination against those who do not have minority status. The Supreme Court agreed. In **Adarand Constructors, Inc. v. Pena**, the Court ruled that affirmative action could make use of quotas or preferences for unqualified persons, and once the program has succeeded, it must be changed or dropped. The controversy continued in the 1990s, and in the **Hopwood v. State of Texas** case (1996), the Supreme Court ruled that any use of race to give an admission to law school was unconstitutional. Also in 1996, Proposition 209 was passed by the voters of California, ended all state-sponsored affirmative action programs. Majority public opinion still seems to favor affirmative action programs, because it is apparent that the effects of discrimination continue today, and perhaps not all discrimination is in the past. [p. 179-181]

Bilingual Education

The rise in recent immigration to this country has created an educational dilemma on how overcome language barriers. Congress authorized bilingual education in 1968 when it passed the Bilingual Education Act. This law was affirmed in the Supreme Court case of **Lau v. Nichols** in 1974. Bilingual education has always been controversial, and with an increased concern about immigration in the 1990s, it has become more controversial. In 1998, California voters passed a law that called for the end of bilingual education programs in the state. [p.181-184]

Special Protection for Older Americans

Age discrimination is potentially the most widespread form of discrimination because it can affect everyone at some point in life. Congress passed the Age Discrimination Employment Act in 1967. This law protects workers over the age of 40, and an amendment to the law passed in 1978 prohibited mandatory retirement of most workers under the age of 70. Older citizens tend to have the highest voter participation, and have created a huge interest group, the American Association of Retired Persons (AARP), to protect their interests. See figure 6-1 for projected elderly population. [p. 184] [p. 184-186]

Securing Rights for Persons with Disabilities

Older Americans and persons with disabilities did not have rights protected by the Civil Rights Act of 1964. The landmark legislation to protect rights of persons with disabilities was the Americans with Disabilities Act of 1990. (ADA) This law requires employers to "reasonably accommodate" the needs of persons with disabilities. This has required physical access, which has led to increased facilities costs for government and business. These costs and the difficulty of interpreting the ADA have caused controversy. In 1998, the Supreme Court ruled that persons infected with HIV, the virus that causes AIDS, are under the protection of the ADA. See figure 6-2 on charges alleging discrimination, [p. 187] [p. 186-188]

The Rights and Status of Gay Males and Lesbians

The "Stonewall Riot" in 1969, in which gays and lesbians fought with police after a raid at a gay bar, created the movement for gay and lesbian rights. The movement has changed state laws on sexual relations between consenting adults, and in a few states and over 150 cities and counties have special laws against gay and lesbian discrimination. The trend toward a more balanced view of state laws to prevent gay and lesbian rights ended in 1986 with the Supreme Court decision in **Bowers v. Hardwick**. This case upheld a Georgia law that made homosexual conduct between two adults a crime. The growth of the political activity of gays has not escaped the notice of politicians. Conservatives have generally been against gay rights, while liberals like Jesse Jackson have supported gay rights. President Clinton in 1997 became the first sitting president to address a gay rights organization. President Clinton was a leading force in developing a "Don't Ask, Don't Tell" policy to allow gays and lesbians to have careers in the military. Probably, the most controversial aspect of gay rights is same-sex marriages and child custody issues. The Hawaii Supreme Court seems to have cleared the way for same-sex marriages in Hawaii. Other states have passed laws banning these marriages. In 1996, Congress passed the Defense of Marriage Act, which bans federal recognition of same-sex marriages. [p. 189-192]

The Rights and Status of Juveniles

Children, defined as persons under the age sixteen, and in some cases under 18 or 21, have generally not had the same legal protection as adults. The reason for this lack of protections is the assumption by society, that their parents basically protect children. The Supreme Court began a slow evolution of children's rights with the **Brown v. Board of Education of Topeka** case, which was fully discussed in Chapter 5. The Brown case granted children the status of rights-bearing persons. In **Yoder v. Wisconsin** in 1972, the Court ruled, "children are 'persons' within the meaning of the Bill of Rights". The Twenty-sixth Amendment to the U.S. Constitution, which was ratified in 1971, granted the right to vote to citizens who are eighteen years old. The fact that eighteen years olds could be drafted and sent to fight and possibly die in Vietnam, seemed to be a key factor in lowering the voting age. In civil and criminal cases, the age of majority, which is the right to manage one's own affairs, and have full enjoyment of civil rights, will vary from eighteen to twenty-one years, depending on the state. In criminal cases, the concept of common law is that children from 7 to 14 years cannot commit a crime because they are not mature enough to understand what they are doing. Recent heinous crimes, such as the shooting deaths of four students and a teacher at a school in Jonesboro, Arkansas, by an 11 year old and a 13 year old, have caused some state officials to consider lowering the age at which a juvenile may be tried as an adult, and faced with adult penalties, including the death penalty. [p. 193-196]

Civil Rights-Beyond Equal Protection: Why Are They Important Today?

While the quest for equal rights has made progress, the struggle is far from over. The expanding proportion of the population that is over the age of sixty-five, will continue to struggle against age discrimination. Persons with disabilities will continue to find new areas of employment, and physical access that will challenge the definitions of the Americans with disabilities Act. Clearly, discrimination continues against gay and lesbian persons, and needs to be addressed. The debate of the rights of children will continue as the nation struggles with the problems of child abuse, and violent crimes committed on others by children. [p. 196-197]

KEY TERMS

affirmative action – p. 179
civil law – p. 194
common law – p.195
criminal law – p. 194
majority – p. 194

mandatory retirement – p. 185
necessaries – p. 194
reverse discrimination – p. 180

OTHER RESOURCES

A number of valuable supplements are available to students using the Schmidt, Shelley, and Bardes text. The full list of the supplements is in the preface to this study guide. Ask your instructor how to obtain these resources. One supplement is highlighted here, the INFOTRAC Online Library.

INFOTRAC EXERCISES

Log on to http://www.infotrac-college.com.
Enter your Pass code that came with your textbook.
Use the CD that came with your textbook for suggestions for articles in this chapter.

PRACTICE EXAM
(Answers appear at the end of this chapter.)

Fill-in-the-Blank. Supply the missing word(s) or term to complete the sentence.

1. The issue of _____ _____ was decided in the case of Bakke v. University of California regents.

2. The Hopwood case brought an end to _____ _____ programs at the University of Texas.

3. California's proposition 209 passed in 1996 ended all _____ _____ programs in that state.

4. The right to a bilingual education was decided in the case of _____ v. _____ in 1974.

5. Initially, the Age Discrimination in Employment Act did not address the issue of _____ _____..

6. The most significant federal legislation with respect to the rights of persons with disabilities is the _____ _____ _____ Act.

7. The Stonewall incident marked the beginning of the movement for _____ ____ _____ _____.

8. The "don't ask, don't tell" policy is directed at _____ and _____ in the military.

9. The reason for the lack of rights in our society for children is the presumption that children are protected by their _____.

10. Common law generally assumes that children under _____ _____ cannot understand the wrongful nature of a crime that they committed.

True/False Circle the appropriate letter to indicate if the statement is true or false.

T   F   1. Affirmative Action is a policy to "level the playing field" for groups that have been discriminated against in the past.

T   F   2. The Bakke case declared affirmative action unconstitutional in any form.

T   F   3. The Proposition 209 in California ended all tax exemptions for citizens over 65 years old.

T   F   4. "English-immersion" programs have replaced bilingual education in some states.

T   F   5. Mandatory retirement rules are now outlawed, except for a few select cases.

T   F   6.   Individuals with AIDS are covered under the American with Disabilities Act of 1990.

T   F   7.   Perhaps the most sensitive political issue with respect to the rights of gay and lesbian couples is whether they should be allowed to marry.

T   F   8.   The Supreme Court has ruled that children are "persons" within the meaning of the Bill of Rights.

T   F   9.   Since the passage of the 26th Amendment, 18 to 20 year olds have had the highest voting turnout of any age group.

T   F   10. If an individual is legally a minor, he or she cannot be held responsible for any contracts signed.

Multiple Choice   Circle the correct response.

1.   The policy steps taken to overcome the present effects of past discrimination is called
     a.   affirmative action.
     b.   legal justification.
     c.   equalizing lawsuit.
     d.   statutory worth.

2.   The ruling of the Supreme Court in the Bakke case
     a.   eliminated all affirmative action in higher education.
     b.   upheld all affirmative action in higher education.
     c.   eliminated racial quotas in affirmative action.
     d.   upheld the use of racial quotas in affirmative action.

3.   The case which directly challenged the Bakke decision was the
     a.   Hopwood v. State of Texas.
     b.   Lau v. Nichols.
     c.   Bowers v. Hardwick.
     d.   Wisconsin v. Yoder.

4.   The concept of "English-immersion" is a direct challenge to
     a.   the rights of the disabled.
     b.   the rights of older Americans.
     c.   bilingual education.
     d.   the rights of juveniles.

5.   The problems of aging and retirement are going to become increasingly important national issues because
     a.   the President and Congress are getting older.
     b.   the population is steadily growing older.
     c.   nursing home owners are such a powerful national lobby.
     d.   the elderly are taking jobs from younger workers.

6.   Mandatory retirement rules
     a.   were prohibited by the Civil Rights Act of 1964.
     b.   were prohibited by the Civil Rights Act of 1991.
     c.   were prohibited by an amendment to the Age Discrimination in Employment Act.
     d.   still apply to most professions, including teaching.

7. Voter participation, used as a measure of political involvement, illustrates that
    a. younger voters are very active.
    b. voting reaches a peak in middle-age and then declines.
    c. older voters participate in the highest percentages.
    d. there are more older people than the other age groups, so they have more voters.

8. The Americans with Disabilities Act requires
    a. the hiring of unqualified job applicants with disabilities.
    b. free public transportation for individuals with disabilities.
    c. "reasonable accommodation" to the needs of persons with disabilities.
    d. free medical insurance for individuals with disabilities.

9. The ruling in the case of Bowers v. Hardwick provided that
    a. same-sex individuals could legally marry
    b. anti-gay legislation is unconstitutional.
    c. homosexual conduct between adults is a crime.
    d. special laws protecting gay and lesbian rights are constitutional.

10. The concept of same-sex marriages is
    a. legal in the state of Vermont
    b. prohibited in all states by the 1996 Defense of Marriage Act passed by Congress.
    c. not legal under the U.S. Constitution.
    d. legal under the "don't ask, don't tell" policy of President Clinton.

11. The first President to address a gay rights organization was
    a. President Truman
    b. President Nixon
    c. President Bush
    d. President Clinton

12. The nation, which recently legalized same-sex marriage is
    a. United States
    b. England
    c. Germany
    d. Netherlands

13. Child custody and adoption by gay men and lesbians is
    a. Illegal in the United States
    b. Illegal in all states
    c. Legal in 22 states
    d. Still being decided by the Supreme Court

14. The reason for the lack of protection for the rights of children is the presumption of our society and lawmakers that children
    a. need no protection.
    b. have all the laws necessary for their protection.
    c. do not need government interfering in their lives.
    d. are basically protected by their parents.

15. The age of majority for a person is
    a. 16 years old
    b. 18 years old
    c. 21 years old
    d. variable from 18 to 21 depending on the state.

16. The aim of the juvenile court system is to
    a. punish by incarceration of the offending youth
    b. hold the youthful offender, until they can be tried as an adult
    c. teach good human contact.
    d. reform rather than to punish the youthful offender.

17. A juvenile's rights in a criminal case are
    a. the same as an adult.
    b. the same as their parents.
    c. limited, unless the judge determines they should be tried as adults.
    d. determined by their age.

18. Zero-Tolerance policies in public school districts usually refer to
    a. cutting class
    b. obscene dress
    c. violent acts
    d. failing standardized state exams

19. The age at which juveniles can be charged with a crime is usually based on
    a. State law
    b. The 14th Amendment
    c. Common law
    d. The American Bar Association

20. Which President first advocated affirmative action?
    a. Lyndon Johnson
    b. George H. Bush
    c. Bill Clinton
    d. Jimmy Carter

Short Essay Questions   Briefly address the major concepts raised by the following questions.

1. Examine the concept of affirmative action. Discuss the important Supreme Court cases defining this concept.

2. Explain the major issues that concern older Americans.

3. Describe the current rights of juveniles in both civil and criminal areas.

4. Explain the rights and status of gay and lesbian individuals in our society. Discuss the important cases or laws.

ANSWERS TO THE PRACTICE EXAM

Fill-in-the-blank

1. reverse discrimination   [p. 180]
2. affirmative action   [p. 180]
3. affirmative action   [p. 180]
4. Lau v. Nichols   [p. 183]
5. mandatory retirement   [p. 185]
6. Americans with Disabilities   [p. 186]
7. gay and lesbian rights   [p. 189]
8. gay and lesbians   [p. 191]
9. parents   [p. 193]
10. 14 years old   [p. 195]

True/False

1. T [p. 179]	3. F [p. 180]	5. T [p. 185]	7. T [p. 191]	9. F [p. 194]
2. F [p. 180]	4. T [p. 183]	6. T [p. 187]	8. T [p. 194]	10. T [p. 194]

Multiple Choice.

1. a [p. 179]	6. c [p. 185]	11. d [p. 190]	16. d [p. 196]
2. c [p. 180]	7. c [p. 185]	12. d [p. 193]	17. c [p. 196]
3. a [p. 180]	8. c [p. 186}	13. c [p. 192]	18. c [p. 196]
4. c [p. 183]	9. c [p. 189]	14. d [p. 193]	19. c [p. 195]
5. b [p. 184]	10. b [p. 191]	15. d [p. 194]	20. a [p. 179]

Short Essay.

An adequate short answer consists of several paragraphs that relate to concepts addressed by the question. Always demonstrate your knowledge of the ideas by giving examples. The following represent major ideas that should be included in the short essay answer.

1. Examine the concept of affirmative action. Discuss the important Supreme Court cases defining this concept. [p. 179-181]

    *   Affirmative action is special consideration or treatment to disadvantaged groups in an effort to overcome present effects of past discrimination.

    *   *Bakke v. University of California regents* (1978) ruled on the concept of reverse discrimination against those who do not have minority status. The Court ruled that specific quotas are unconstitutional, but affirmative action was constitutional.

    *   *Hopwood v. State of Texas* (1996) ruled that race and other factors could not be used for determining admission to professional school. This case basically ruled existing affirmative action programs unconstitutional.

    *   Proposition 209, passed in California in 1996, ended all state-sponsored affirmative action programs.

2. Explain the major issues that concern older Americans [p. 184-186].

   • Age discrimination is potentially the most widespread form of discrimination because anyone could be a victim at some point in his or her life.

   • Older Americans are very concerned about losing their jobs to younger, lower-salaried workers.

   • The Age Discrimination in Employment Act of 1967 (ADEA) gave protection to older workers. Originally the Act did not protect workers from mandatory retirement, but this was added by amendment in 1978.

   • Older Americans are very concerned about Social Security and medical benefits. They have formed a huge interest group (AARP) to maintain spending for these programs.

3. Describe the current rights of juveniles in both civil and criminal areas. [p. 194-196]

   • Juveniles do not have the legal rights of adults because it is assumed that parents will protect their children.

   • The Supreme Court in *Yoder v. Wisconsin* (1972) ruled that children are "persons" under the meaning of the Bill of Rights.

   • The rights of juveniles depend upon the age of majority. This concept means the age at which a person is entitled by law to manage his or her own affairs and have full civil rights. This varies from 18 to 21 years old depending upon the state.

   • In Civil cases, juveniles cannot be held responsible for contracts, unless it is for necessaries (things necessary for subsistence as determined by the court).

   • In Criminal cases, juveniles do not have the same due process rights as adults, but usually do not face the same penalties. In common law, it is presumed that children under fourteen do not understand the nature of their crimes. Recent mass murders by children under fourteen at a school in Jonesboro, Arkansas, have challenged the concept of when a child may be tried as an adult and receive adult punishment, even the death penalty.

4. Explain the rights and status of gay and lesbian individuals in our society. Discuss the important cases or laws. [p. 189-193]

   • The 1969 Stonewall riot at a New York City gay bar marked the beginning of the gay and lesbian rights movement.

   • During the 1970s and 1980s many state and local laws against gays and lesbian were repealed.

   • In *Bowers v. Hardwick* (1986), however, the Supreme Court ruled that state laws prohibiting homosexual contact between adults were constitutional. In *Romer v. Evans* (1996), the Court ruled that states could not pass laws that take all legal protections from homosexuals.

   • President Clinton established a "don't ask, don't tell" policy to allow gays and lesbians to have careers in the military. This policy has been controversial and has critics on both sides of the debate.

   • In 1996, the Hawaii Supreme Court cleared the way for same-sex marriages in that state. This controversy has been even greater than the issue of homosexuals serving in military. Congress, in the Defense of Marriage Act, and at least 16 states and have passed laws banning same-sex marriages.

   • Child-custody rights are also difficult for gay and lesbian parents.

Chapter 7
PUBLIC OPINION AND POLITICAL SOCIALIZATION

CHAPTER SUMMARY

Public opinion clearly plays an important role in our political system. President George W. Bush has had widespread support for his war of terrorism. Two other presidents have shown just how powerful public opinion can be. Opposition to the War in Vietnam seemed to be a factor in 1968, when President Lyndon Johnson declined to run for re-election. Public opinion on the scandal surrounding the 1972 Watergate break-in gave Congress strong support to initiate impeachment proceeding against President Nixon. [p. 205]

Defining Public Opinion

Public opinion is defined as the aggregate of individual attitudes or beliefs shared by some portion of adults. Public opinion is made known in a democracy by protests, demonstrations, and lobbying by interest groups. There are very few issues on which most Americans agree. When a large proportion of the public does appear to hold the same view on an issue, a consensus exists. If opinion is polarized between two quite different positions, divisive opinion exists. Nonopinion is where a large number of people have no opinion. See Figure 7-1,7-2, and Figure 7-3 p. 206, for examples of each of these concepts.

Measuring Public Opinion

One of the most common means of gathering and measuring public opinion is through the use of opinion polls. In the 1800s, newspapers and magazines used face-to-face straw polls to attract readers. In the 20th century, the magazine *Literary Digest* developed modern techniques by mailing questionnaires to subscribers. In 1936, the magazine's poll predicted that Alfred Landon would defeat Franklin Roosevelt for President. Landon won only two states. The most important principle in poll taking is randomness [p. 208]. If drawn from a truly random sample of opinions, a poll should be relatively accurate. Gallup and Roper polls interview about 1,500 individuals to get within a margin of error of 3%. [p. 209]. See Table 7-1 for the margins of error since 1936. Public opinion polls are snapshots of opinions at a specific time on a specific question. The timing of the poll, a sampling error of interviewing too few people, and the wording of the question, can all create an inaccurate prediction of a political outcome.

Technology and Opinion Polls

During the 1970's, telephone polling began to dominate over in-person polling. The success of the telemarketing industry has caused a huge no response rate on the telephone. The Internet has replaced the telephone as the latest polling technology. It remains to be seen, if it goes the way of the telephone. [p. 214]

How Public Opinion is Formed: Political Socialization

The process by which individuals acquire political beliefs and opinion is called political socialization. The most important influence in this process is the family. Children have a strong need for parental approval, and are very receptive to the parent's opinions. The clearest family influence is the political party identification. [p. 215] Schools are also an important influence. Education seems to influence the level of activity in the political process. The more education a person receives the higher the level of political activity. Friendships and associations in peer groups can influence political attitudes. Religious associations also create political attitudes, although this is hard to measure. In recent years, over 42% of evangelical Protestants are Republicans. Wealth and social status influence political attitudes, although there is probably a strong correlation with the education factor in shaping wealth and social status. When events produce a long-term political impact, you have generational effects, which can influence political opinions. For example, voters who grew up in the 1930s during the Great Depression were likely to become Democrats. Some individuals have the ability to influence the opinions of others because of position, expertise or personality. Often these individuals, called opinion leaders, use the media to influence opinions. Finally, the election of Ronald Reagan in 1980 seemed to produce a gender gap, in which women were 5 or 6% more likely to vote for Democrats for President. This gap continues into 2000s [p. 216-219].

Political Culture and Public Opinion

Although Americans are divided into numerous ethnic, religious, political groups, the American political culture binds us together with the core values of (1) liberty, equality, and property; (2) support for religion;

and (3) community service and personal achievement. Another important element is the trust that individuals express in the government and political institutions. Unfortunately, trust in political institutions reached an all time low in 1992. See Table 7-2 on page 220.

Public Opinion about Government

Public opinion about the confidence in various institutions in our society has declined in the 1990s. Church and bank are lower than previous decades. The military and Supreme Court are government institutions that have the highest levels of confidence. See Table 7-3 on page 221. While the public may have little confidence in some government institutions, they still turn to government to solve major problems. See Table 7-4 page 222. While the exact influence of public opinion on government policy cannot be measured, it appears that politicians, who ignore public opinion, run a great risk of defeat in the next election.

Public Opinion: Why Is It Important Today?

Public opinion is a vital part of the political process. The over use of polls and poll results in the media seem to have caused a public reaction against this process. The sample of individuals willing to provide poll data is declining. This could be a dangerous trend, which makes it more difficult to accurately judge opinions on the serious issues affecting our society. [p. 223]

KEY TERMS

consensus—p. 206
divisive opinion—p. 206
gender gap—p. 219
generational effect —p. 217
media—p. 218
opinion leader—p. 217

opinion poll—p. 207
peer group—p. 216
political socialization—p. 215
political trust—p. 220
public opinion—p. 206
sampling error—p. 210

OTHER RESOURCES

A number of valuable supplements are available to students using the Schmidt, Shelley, and Bardes text. The full list of the supplements is in the preface to this study guide. Ask your instructor how to obtain these resources. One supplement is highlighted here, the INFOTRAC Online Library.

INFOTRAC EXERCISES

Log on to http://www.infotrac-college.com.
Enter your Pass code that came with your textbook.
Use the CD that came with your textbook for suggestions for articles in this chapter.

PRACTICE EXAM
[Answers appear at the end of this chapter.]

Fill-in-the-Blank. Supply the missing word(s) or term(s) to complete the sentence.

1. The aggregate of individual attitudes and beliefs is _____ _____.

2. How much people will express their opinions determines when private opinion becomes _____ _____.

3. _____ _____ is polarized between two quite different positions.

4. One of the most common ways of gathering public opinion is _____ _____.

5. When a large proportion of the American public expresses the same view on an issue, we say that a _____ exists.

6. Roper. Gallup, and Crossley developed modern polling techniques to predict the total voting population by using _____ _____ with small samples of selected voters.

7. The most important principle in sampling public opinion is _____.

8. The _____ is the most important influence in political socialization.

9. _____ _____ is the term that describes the differences in issue orientation and voting behavior between men and women.

10. Politicians tend to make decisions based on _____ benefits to his or her constituents.

True/False. Circle the appropriate letter to indicate if the statement is true or false.

T   F   1. Adverse public opinion in 1968 caused President Johnson to decline to run for re-election.

T   F   2. Nonopinion is when most Americans have no information on an issue.

T   F   3. Quota sampling is a more accurate technique for public opinion than random sampling.

T   F   4. Children accept their parents' political attitudes because of communication and receptivity.

T   F   5. Education has little to do with interest or activity in politics.

T   F   6. During the 1960s and 1970s, political trust declined steeply.

T   F   7. Generational effects can result in long-lasting attachments to political parties.

T   F   8. The government institution the public has the most confidence in today, is the military.

T   F   9. Election research suggests that policymakers are responsive to public opinion.

T   F   10. Well-defined public opinion tends to restrain government officials from taking unpopular actions.

Multiple-Choice. Circle the correct response.

1. The aggregate of individual attitudes or beliefs shared by some portion of adults is referred to as
    a. political opinion.
    b. Propaganda.
    c. public opinion.
    d. an ideology.

2. General agreement among the citizenry on an issue is called
    a. propaganda.
    b. public opinion.
    c. consensus.
    d. political rhetoric

3. When public opinion is polarized between two quite different positions it is said to be
    a. consensus
    b. divisive
    c. private
    d. in error

4. The Literary Digest polling activities was an example of
    a. modern polling techniques
    b. the use of exit interviews
    c. a nonrepresentative sample
    d. telephone interviews

5. The most important principle in sampling is
    a. a large sample
    b. picking an issue where consensus can be found
    c. randomness
    d. asking the right questions

6. Sampling error is the difference between the sample result and the
    a. eligible voters
    b. likely voters
    c. true result
    d. biased result

7. Support for civil liberties and tolerance of different points of view is highest among
    a. people influenced by peer groups
    b. people influenced by religious associations
    c. people of lower economic status
    d. people of higher economic status

8. Push polls are
    a. the most accurate opinion polls
    b. used by candidates to influence voters
    c. used by television reporters
    d. like quota sampling

9. The most important influence on political socialization is
    a. peer group
    b. family
    c. political events
    d. education

10. A person's place of residence seems to effect political attitudes, with big city dwellers tending to be
    a. liberal and Democratic
    b. liberal and Republican
    c. conservative and Democratic
    d. conservative and Republican

11. The most important values in the American political system include
    a. federalism, unity, and freedom
    b. support for the president, Congress, and the courts
    c. liberty, equality, and property
    d. the two-party system, and respect for the Constitution

12. Fundamentalist or evangelical Christians tend to support
    a. Democrats
    b. Republicans
    c. Independents
    d. no political parties at all

13. Political events like the Vietnam War tend to produce what are called
    a. peer group influence
    b. social and economic influence
    c. opinion leader influence
    d. generational effects

14. According to studies, which group is mostly likely to use media to form basic political attitudes
    a. the elderly
    b. college graduates
    c. high school students
    d. women

15. The impact of strong public opinion on government action
    a. encourages officials to ignore public opinion
    b. allows government officials to shape policy according to opinion polls
    c. restrains officials from taking truly unpopular actions
    d. discourages public officials from standing up for what is right.

16. The Gallup Report of 2002 listed which of the following as the most important problems?
    a. morals, family decline
    b. economy, education
    c. terrorism, economy
    d. crime, violence

17. The Gender Gap refers to voting in which women voted for
    a. Ronald Reagan
    b. Woman candidates
    c. Republican presidential candidates
    d. Democrat presidential candidates

18. According to political scientists, Page and Shapiro, the government responds to public opinion about
    a. 10 percent of the time
    b. 30 percent of the time
    c. half (50) percent of the time
    d. two-thirds of the time

19. Although people do not have much confidence in government institutions, polls show that they
    a. expect government to solve major problems
    b. expect nonprofits to solve major problems
    c. expect individuals to solve major problems by dropping out of society
    d. avoid thinking about problems

20. Which of the following statements about public opinion polls is correct?
    a. public opinion polls lead to direct policy change.
    b. public opinion polls do not identify issues important to the public.
    c. public opinion polls are not very important in the political process today.
    d. public opinion polls do identify issues important to the public.

Short Essay Questions. Briefly address the major concepts raised by the following questions.

1. Define the qualities of public opinion.

2. Describe the key factors in conducting opinion polls.

3. Explain the most important influences in political socialization.

4. Discuss the most important values of the American political system and the trends of political trust in the last three decades.

ANSWERS TO THE PRACTICE EXAM

Fill-in-the-Blank.

1.	public opinion	[p. 206]
2.	public opinion	[p. 206]
3.	divisive opinion	[p. 206]
4.	opinion polls	[p. 207]
5.	consensus	[p. 206]
6.	personal interviews	[p. 207]
7.	randomness	[p. 208]
8.	family	[p. 215]
9.	gender gap	[p. 219]
10.	net	[p. 223]

True/False

1.	T	[p. 205]	3.	F	[p. 208]	5.	F	[p. 216]	7. T [p. 217]	9. T [p. 221]
2.	T	[p. 206]	4.	T	[p. 215]	6.	T	[p. 220]	8. T [p. 221]	10. T [p. 222]

Multiple Choice.

1.	c	[p. 206]	6.	c	[p. 210]	11. c	[p. 220]	16. c [p. 222]	
2.	c	[p. 206]	7.	d	[p. 217]	12. b	[p. 216]	17. d [p. 219]	
3.	b	[p. 206]	8.	b	[p. 211]	13. d	[p. 217]	18. d [p. 222]	
4.	c	[p. 207]	9.	b	[p. 215]	14. c	[p. 218]	19. a [p. 221]	
5.	c	[p. 208]	10.	a	[p. 219]	15. c	[p. 222]	20. d [p. 223]	

Short Essay Answers.

An adequate short answer consists of several paragraphs that discuss the concepts addressed by the question. Always demonstrate your knowledge of the ideas by giving examples. The following represent major ideas that should be included in these short essays.

1. Define public opinion [p. 206].
   - The aggregate of individual attitudes or beliefs shared by some portion of the adult population.
   - Consensus opinion is general agreement among the citizenry on an issue.
   - Divisive opinion is public opinion that is polarized between two quite different positions.
   - Nonopinion is where people probably won't know much about it or are not interested enough to formulate a position..

2. Describe the key factors in conducting opinion polls [p. 207-212]. There are three key factors in conducting accurate public opinion polls.

   - Randomness is the most important factor. The sample to be interviewed must be representative of the whole population. One technique is to choose a random sample of telephone numbers. A quota sampling, which is not as accurate, is to select people who represent certain types of people. The major polls can interview about 1,500 people and predict elections within a margin of three percent, plus or minus.
   - Timing is a second factor. Polls continue to be conducted until the election day because a shift in opinion at the last minute can produce an unexpected outcome. The polls in the presidential election of 1980 between Carter and Reagan showed a very close contest. Reagan won easily, because of a shift in the undecided vote in the last week of the election.
   - The types of questions asked on the survey have a major impact on the results of the poll. If poorly worded or leading questions are asked, the result will be distorted.

3. Explain the most important influences in political socialization [p. 215-219]. Political socialization is the process by which individuals acquire political beliefs and attitudes.

   - The family is the most important influence and largely responsible for political party choice.
   - Schools are most likely to influence the understanding of issues and political activity.
   - Peer groups most strongly influence direct involvement in political activity.
   - Religion has some impact on political activity, but its influence is not clear.
   - Wealth and social-class influence a tolerance for differences and more voting activity.
   - Generational events, such as the great Depression, can influence opinion for decades.
   - Charismatic opinion leaders using the power of media can have a tremendous impact on opinion.
   - The demographic factors of age, gender, location, and region of residence have the final influences on the process we call political socialization.

4. Discuss the most important values of the American political system and the trend in political trust over the last three decades [p. 219-223]. The core elements of the American political system include:

   - Liberty, equality, and property.
   - Support for religion.
   - Community service and personal achievement.
   - These generally-supported values provide an environment of support for the political system, which helps the system survive a crisis such as scandal. The levels of political trust that citizens have in the system declined tremendously in the 1960s and 1970s and reached an all-time low in 1992. The military and the Supreme Court are the most trusted parts of the political system today.

Chapter 8
INTEREST GROUPS

CHAPTER SUMMARY
The role of interest groups in the American political process can be illustrated by their activities with respect to legislation passed by Congress after the September 11 attacks on the World Trade Center and the Pentagon. [p. 231]

Interest Groups: A Natural Phenomenon
Pluralist theory discussed in chapter 1, advocates that the structure of American government invites a political process in which interest groups compete with each other. Famed French visitor, Alexis de Tocqueville observed in 1834, that American seemed to be a nation of joiners of associations. Interest groups are often created from mass social movements, which represent the demands of a large segment of the population for major social change. The Civil Rights movement of the 1950s and 1960s is a good example of a social movement. p. [231-234]

Why Do Americans Join Interest Groups?
According to the theory of Mancur Olson, it is not rational for individuals to join groups. If a group is successful in getting some benefit, how can that benefit be denied to others in the same situation? Why pay union dues, if workers benefits achieved by the union go to all workers? It is more logical to wait for others to gain benefits and then share them. People need incentives to join groups. The three major incentives are solidary, material and purposive. Solidary incentives include companionship, a sense of belonging, and the pleasure of associating together. Material incentives are of course economic benefits or opportunities. Purposive incentives relate to ones ethical beliefs or ideological principles. [p. 234-235]

Types of Interest Groups
Although thousands of groups exist to influence government, they can be discussed in a few broad categories. See Table 8-1, p. 237 for characteristics of selected interest groups.

A variety of economic interest groups mirror the complexity of the American economy, and include business, agriculture, labor, public employee, and professional organizations. The largest business groups are the National Association of Manufactures (NAM), U.S. Chamber of Commerce, and the Business Roundtable. American farmers have been very successful lobbying for government support, even though they represent about 2 percent of U.S. workers. The American Farm Bureau and the National Farmers' Union are the most powerful agriculture groups. Labor unions have tired to balance the power of business groups, but have weakened in recent years. The biggest union is the giant AFL-CIO. Public Employee interest groups have grown in recent years. These groups are similar to unions, but lack the legal power to strike, which has not stopped them from strikes. One of the biggest of these unions is the American Federation of State, County, and Municipal Employees (AFSCME). Finally, professional occupations, such as lawyers, and doctors are well represented in the American Bar Association, and American Medical Association. Environmental interest groups actually began in the early part of the century, with the National Audubon Society and the Sierra Club. Mass memberships groups have been created since Earth Day in 1972. These groups include National Wildlife Federation and the Nature Conservancy. Public interest groups, concerned with the public good, have been created almost single-handed by consumer activist, Ralph Nader. Some of the largest public interest groups that have developed without Nader's help are Common Cause and the American Civil Liberties Union. Special interest groups, sometimes called single interest groups, can be very effective because they concentrate resources on a single issue. The National Rifle Association, and the American Association of Retired Persons are good examples of this type of group. Finally, foreign governments of the largest trading partners of the U.S., hire lobbyists to try to influence trade policy. Japan, South Korea, Canada, and the European Union (EU) are just a few of the foreign government interest groups. {p. 237-243}

What Makes an Interest Group Powerful?
There are four factors, which allow interest groups to attain a reputation for being powerful. These are their membership size, leadership, financial resources, and cohesiveness. [p. 243-244]

Interest Group Strategies
Interest group techniques of influence can be divided into direct techniques, and indirect techniques. The direct techniques use lobbying, publicizing ratings of public officials, and campaign contributions. P. 259. Lobbyists are private citizens who meet public officials on behalf of the interest that they represent. See page 245 for a list of lobbying activities. Many groups will publish the voting records of legislators on issues of interest to the group. Indirect techniques use the general public or individuals to influence the government for the interest group. Interest groups will try to generate a "groundswell" of support through mass mailing and advertising. Climate control is a similar concept, where organizations will use public relation techniques to try to create favorable public opinion about a group or industry. Another effective indirect technique is use constituents to lobby the lawmaker. The "shotgun" approach tries to get as many people as possible to write or call or E-mail. In the "rifle" approach, the group tries to get a few influential constituents to talk to the lawmaker. A final indirect technique is to form an alliance with other groups that are concerned with the same legislation. [p. 244-248]

Interest Groups and Campaign Money
The major technique of the last twenty years to directly influence is the creation of Political Action Committees (PAC). These PACs, which have grown to over 4,500 in the 1990s, are a major source of campaign contributions to candidates. See Figure 8-2 and 8-3, p. 249 for the growth and contributions to Congressional candidates from 1985 to 2000. See table 8-2 and 8-3, p. 250 which provide names and amounts of PAC contributions. In addition to PAC's, soft money, and issue advocacy advertising have been major influences in recent years. [p. 248-252]

Regulating Lobbyists
The first attempt to regulate lobbyists and lobbying activities was the Legislative Reorganization Act of 1946. This law was ruled constitutional in the Supreme Court case of United States v. Harriss in 1954. The Court upheld a narrow interpretation of the law, which meant that very few lobbyists actually registered under the law. In 1995, Congress passed a far-reaching lobby regulation law, which should require 3 to ten times as many lobbyists to register. Congress also decided to change rules relating to gifts and travel expenses. See page 252-253 for a list of the major provisions of the law.

Interest Groups and Representative Democracy
The role of interest groups in our democracy is a continuing topic of debate. Clearly, members of interest groups are middle or upper class in background. Leaders of interest groups can be called an "elite within an elite", because often they are from a higher social class than the members of the group. Pluralist theory from chapter 1 presumes that groups compete with each other for the benefit of the members, but there is a very strong presence of elites in this picture, which is Elite theory from chapter 1. In the overall analysis of interest groups, it is clearly that even the most powerful group does not always prevail. By definition, an interest group can only be effective on a narrow range of interests, which hold the group together. When groups try to deal with broad policy issues, they fragment their membership base, and cannot influence policy. [p. 253-254]

Interest Groups: Why Are They Important Today?
The role of interest groups in American society has been debated since the writing of the Constitution. James Madison warned us in the Federalists Papers about the "spirit of faction". The debate for the future seems to be focused on the issue of campaign contributions by interest groups. One possible solution is public financing, which is used in the Presidential election. Groups will continue to prosper in the future, as they provide real opportunities for more and more citizens to participate in the political process, and to influence public policy toward their interest. [p. 254]

KEY TERMS

Climate control - p. 247
Direct technique - p. 245
Indirect technique - p. 245
Interest group - p. 231
Lobbyist - p. 231
Material incentive - p. 235

Political action committee (PAC) - p. 248
Public interest - p. 241
Purposive incentive - p. 235
Service sector - p. 239
Social movement - p. 233
Solidary incentive - p. 234

OTHER RESOURCES

A number of valuable supplements are available to students using the Schmidt, Shelley, and Bardes text. The full list of the supplements is in the preface to this study guide. Ask your instructor how to obtain these resources. One supplement is highlighted here, the INFOTRAC Online Library.

INFOTRAC EXERCISES

Log on to http://www.infotrac-college.com.
Enter your Pass code that came with your textbook.
You can access the article by typing the exact phrase below.

Environmental Groups
Think Locally, Act Globally.
The premise of this article is the protest in Seattle against the World Trade Organization (WTO) was a coming-out party of "global forces of labor and environmental movements.

Study Questions
1.   Why was the protest in Seattle such a surprise?
2.   What is the concept of small groups?
3.   What kind of global society is evolving?

Lobbying
Letters, We Get Letters
Grassroot Lobbying
The premise of this article is face-to-face encounters with office holders is much more effective than letters.

Study Questions
1.   Have you ever written a letter to an office holder?
2.   Have you ever had a face-to-face encounter with an office holder?
3.   Which approach do you think is more effective?

Campaign Contributions
How Become Top Banana
The premise of this article is Carl Linder Jr., a multimillionaire banana baron wanted to conquer more of the European market. He was able to influence the U.S. government to launch a trade war for him. A number of small businesses were hurt as a result.

Study Questions
1.   How does this article tie into the concept of a global society from article one?
2.   Why does Linder give campaign contributions to both Democrats and Republicans?
3.   Were you surprised at how much money can be contributed to government officials?

Campaign Contributions
Mother's Milk, Elections
The premise of this article is "money is the mother's milk of politics" Money has always been a factor in American elections. Each election cycle seems to cost more and more money.

Study Questions
1. What did the case of Buckley v. Valeo decide?
2. What is "soft money?
3. What are the current trends in campaign financing?

PRACTICE EXAM
(Answers appear at the end of this chapter.)

Fill-in-the-Blank. Supply the missing word(s) or term to complete the sentence.

1. An interest group must give individuals a _____ to become members.

2. _____ _____ represent the demands of a large segment of the public for social change.

3. Numerous interest groups in the United States have been formed to promote _____ interests.

4. In spite of representing about 2% of the population, _____ interest groups have been very successful in receiving government aid.

5. Since 1965, the degree of unionization of the _____ sector has declined, but this has been offset by the growth of unionization of _____ employees.

6. Consumer activist, _____ _____, has organized the most well known public interest groups.

7. The nations largest interest group is the _____ _____ _____ _____.

8. The techniques used by interest groups may be divided into those that are _____ and _____.

9. Within the last two decades, the most important form of campaign help from groups is the political contribution from a group's _____ _____ _____.

10. _____ _____ is a public relations strategy by an interest group to improve its public image.

True/False   Circle the appropriate letter to indicate if the statement is true or false.

T   F   1. The structure of our political system makes it difficult for individuals and groups to exert influence on the system.

T   F   2. James Madison was a firm believer in strengthening interest group activity.

T   F   3. The strength of union membership has traditionally been in the service sector of the workforce.

T   F   4. Foreign governments are prohibited from lobbying in the United States.

T   F   5. The use of public relations techniques to influence public opinion about a group is called the rifle approach.

T   F   6. In the last twenty years, the influence of political action committees has tended to diminish within the overall campaign process.

T   F   7. One of the most effective interest group activities is the use of constituents to lobby for the group's goals.

T   F   8. Most interest groups have a middle-class or upper-class bias.

T   F   9. The Federal Regulation of Lobbying Act regulates all forms of lobbying at the national level of government.

T   F   10. The existence of interest groups allows individuals to influence government far beyond just voting.

Multiple Choice   Circle the correct response.

1. Any organized group whose members share common objectives and actively attempt to influence the government is a(n)
    a. political party
    b. bureaucracy
    c. interest group
    d. institution

2. It is possible for individuals and groups to exert influence at many different points in our government because
    a. officials are always looking for campaign contributions
    b. interest group members are also voters
    c. of the structure of our political system.
    d. we have a unitary form of government

3. Companionship, a sense of belonging, and the pleasure of associating with others as reasons for belonging to interest groups are referred to as
    a. material incentives
    b. purposive incentives
    c. solidary incentives
    d. herd incentives

4. Interest groups are often spawned by mass
    a. increases of young voters
    b. publication of "underground" newspapers
    c. factionalism
    d. social movements

5. The role of labor unions in American society has weakened in recent years, as witnessed by
    a. the rise of business groups
    b. a decline in union membership
    c. the lack of effective leadership
    d. an increase in government regulation

6. Since 1965, the greatest growth in unionization has occurred in the unionization of
    a. military personnel
    b. professional athletes
    c. public employees
    d. private sector employees

7. Lobbying, ratings of legislative behavior, and campaign assistance are
    a. the main indirect techniques used by interest groups
    b. considered ineffective methods of swaying votes
    c. the main direct techniques used by interest groups
    d. considered obsolete in view of today's modern technology

8. The bulk of campaign contributions from interest groups goes to
    a. presidential candidates
    b. liberals more than conservatives
    c. candidates who face little or no opposition
    d. challengers rather than incumbents

9. The U.S. v Harriss case ruled that the Federal Regulation of Lobbying Act
    a. is constitutional
    b. is unconstitutional
    c. should be left to the states to regulate
    d. only applies to presidential elections

10. The "shotgun" approach to lobbying consists of
    a. mobilizing large numbers of constituents to write or phone their legislators
    b. identifying specific constituents to write or phone their legislators
    c. concentrating only on gun control issues
    d. allowing lobbyists to determine the most appropriate strategy

11. One of the benefits of forming alliances between interest groups is that
    a. it is easier to keep track of interest groups if they are fewer in numbers
    b. it makes it easier to solicit contributions
    c. there is strength in numbers
    d. it shares expenses and multiplies the influence

12. The recent changes of the Federal Regulation of Lobbying Act exempted what kind of lobbyist?
    a. Lobbyists earning less than $200, 000 a year
    b. "grassroot"s lobbyists
    c. all lobbyists
    d. lobbyists spending 40% or less of their time lobbying

13. Interest groups tend to have a(n)
    a. lower class bias
    b. middle to upper-class bias
    c. a neutral bias
    d. a democratic foundation for decision-making

14. The nation's largest interest group is the
    a. American Association of Retired Persons
    b. Common Cause
    c. National Education Association
    d. National Rifle Association

15. The great advantage for democracy in interest group activity is that
    a. it is a way to demonstrate support for governmental policy
    b. individual citizens are empowered to influence government
    c. it serves as a basis of political party organization
    d. it is a way to monitor the activities of Congress

16. Which of the following is not a special one-issue interest group?
    a. National Abortion Rights
    b. National Rifle Association
    c. The Right to Work Committee
    d. AFL-CIO

17. Foreign governments are
    a. banned by the Constitution from lobbying in the U.S.
    b. banned by Congress from lobbying in the U.S.
    c. able to lobby extensively
    d. able to lobby, but rarely do so.

18. The use of public-relation techniques to create favorable public opinion toward an interest group is called
    a. lobbying
    b. rating
    c. climate control
    d. groundswell

19. The theory that views politics as a struggle among interest groups is
    a. elitism
    b. democracy
    c. pluralism
    d. federalism

20. The "founding father" who worried about how to control the "mischiefs of faction" was
    a. Thomas Jefferson
    b. James Madison
    c. George Washington
    d. John Adams

Short Essay Questions   Briefly address the major concepts raised by the following questions.

1. Discuss the incentives for an individual to join an interest group.

2. Describe the various types of major interest groups.

3. Explain the direct techniques used by interest groups to influence government.

4. Discuss the indirect techniques used by interest groups to influence government.

ANSWERS TO THE PRACTICE EXAM

Fill-in-the-blank

1. incentive   [p. 234]
2. social movements   [p. 233]
3. economic   [p. 237]
4. agricultural   [p. 238]
5. private, public   [p. 240]
6. Ralph Nader   [p. 242]
7. American Association of Retired Persons   [p. 243]
8. direct, indirect   [p. 245]
9. Political Action Committees (PAC)   [p. 248]
10. climate control   [p. 247]

True/False

1.	F	[p. 234]	3.	F	[p. 239]	5.	F	[p. 248]	7.	T	[p. 248]	9.	F	[p. 253]
2.	T	[p. 231]	4.	F	[p. 243]	6.	F	[p. 248]	8.	T	[p. 253]	10.	T	[p. 254]

Multiple Choice.

1.	c	[p. 231]	6.	c	[p. 240]	11.	d	[p. 246]	16.	d	[p. 242]
2.	c	[p. 231]	7.	c	[p. 245]	12.	b	[p. 253]	17.	c	[p. 243]
3.	c	[p. 234]	8.	c	[p. 248]	13.	b	[p. 253]	18.	c	[p. 247]
4.	d	[p. 233]	9.	a	[p. 252]	14.	a	[p. 243]	19.	c	[p. 253]
5.	b	[p. 239]	10.	a	[p. 247]	15.	b	[p. 254]	20.	b	[p. 254]

Short Essay.

An adequate short answer consists of several paragraphs that relate to concepts addressed by the question. Always demonstrate your knowledge of the ideas by giving examples. The following represent major ideas that should be included in the short essay answer.

1. Discuss the incentives for an individual to join an interest group. [p. 234-235].
    *   There are three major incentives for individuals to join interest groups, solidary, material, and purposive.
        *   Solidary incentives include companionship, a sense of belonging, and the pleasure of associating with others
        *   Material incentives are economic benefits or opportunities, such as discounts, insurance, or travel planning.
        *   Purposive incentives provide the satisfaction of taking action for one's beliefs or principles.

2. Describe the various types of major interest groups. [p. 235-243].
   - The major types of interest groups are economic, environmental, public, special, and foreign governments.
     - Economic interest groups include business, agricultural, labor, public employees, and professional.
     - Environmental interest groups began in 1905 with the National Audubon society. More recent groups include the National Wildlife Federation, and the Nature Conservancy.
     - Public interest groups were greatly influenced by consumer activist Ralph Nader. One of the largest public interest groups today is Common Cause.
     - Special interest groups, or single-interest groups, focus on one issue such as for and against abortion or gun control.
     - Foreign governments that are major trading partners of the U.S. lobby for trade concessions and aid from the U.S. government.

3. Explain the direct techniques used by interest groups to influence government. [p. 245-246].
   - There are three important direct techniques of interest group influence. These are lobbying, rating of legislators, and campaign assistance.
     - Lobbying entails a range of activities, which include private meetings, testifying in public meetings, drafting legislation, providing political information, and influencing during social occasions.
     - Rating of legislators on specific votes on issues important to the group provides the members of the group with important information on which candidates to vote for.
     - Campaign assistance in the form of campaign contribution has grown tremendously in the past two decades, because of the increase in the number of Political Action Committees (PAC). PACs account for about one-third of all campaign contributions.

4. Discuss the indirect techniques used by interest groups to influence government. [p. 247-248].
   - Indirect techniques allow interest groups to influence government policy by using the general public, individual constituents, and other interest groups.
     - Interest groups try to create a "groundswell" of public opinion by using mass advertising. Sometimes, public relations techniques are used to create favorable public opinion toward the interest. This technique is known as climate control.
     - The use of individual constituents is one of the most successful techniques. The attempt to mobilize as many constituents as possible is know as the "shotgun" approach. An attempt to mobilize very influential constituents is called the "rifle" approach.
     - Building an alliance with other interest groups on common issues, allows groups to share costs and multiple their influence.

Chapter 9
POLITICAL PARTIES

CHAPTER SUMMARY

What is a Political Party?

A political party is a group of political activists who organize to win elections, to operate the government, and to determine public policy. A faction is a group that acts together in pursuit of some special interest. [p. 261].

Function of Political Parties in the United States

Political parties have five basic functions. These are: (1) recruiting candidates for public office, (2) organizing and running elections, (3) presenting alternative policies, (4) accepting responsibility for operating the government, and (5) acting as the organized opposition to the party in power. [p. 261-262].

A Short History of Political Parties in the United States

The evolution of our political party system can be divided into six periods. The first period from 1789 to 1812 was the creation of political parties. The Federalists pushed for adoption of the Constitution, and the Anti-Federalists were against adoption. The second period from 1816 to 1824 was the era of personal politics, because elections centered on individual candidates rather than parties. The third period of Andrew Jackson's presidency to the Civil War, from 1828-1860, saw the birth and death of the Whig party. The fourth period from 1864 to 1892 was the creation of the heavily Democratic South, and the heavily Republican North. The next period from 1896 to 1928 saw the development of the Progressive Party, which ran Theodore Roosevelt for President in 1912. The final period was the modern era from 1932 to the present. The new deal of President Franklin Roosevelt created the basic landscape of politics that we have today. [p. 262-267]. See Figure 9-1 Page 263 for a look at the different political parties in the U.S. from 1789.

The Three Faces of a Party

Each political party consists of three major components. These are; the party-in-the-electorate, which are people who express a preference for one party over the other, the party organization, which are structure, staff, and official members of the party, and the party-in-government, who are the elected and appointed government officials. [p. 267-268].

Party Organization

American political parties have a standard, pyramid-shaped organization. The national party organization consists of the national convention, which selects the national committee, and national chairperson to direct the party during the four-year period between the national conventions. See table 9-1, p. 269 for a look at the votes of national convention delegates in 2000.

The state party organization consists of a state committee, state chairperson, and a number of local organizations. States parties are important in national politics because of the unit rule, which allots electoral votes in an indivisible bloc except in Maine and Nebraska. The lowest level of party organization, called the grass roots, is composed of county and district party officials, precinct chairpersons, and party workers. The political machine no longer exists because of the decline of patronage. Local political organization can still have a major impact on elections, particularly local elections. [p. 268-272].

The Two Major U.S. Parties and their Members

The core of the Democratic Party is minorities, the working class, and various ethnic groups. Democrats generally support government intervention in the economy to help individuals in need. The Republican Party draws its support from college graduates, upper-income families, and professionals or businesspersons. Republicans support the private marketplace, and feel that the government should be involved in fewer social programs. [p. 272-274]. See Figure 9-2, page 273 for a survey on which party is better at various policy areas.

Why Has the Two-Party System Endured?

There are a number of factors that explain why the United States has a two-party system. The historical development of political parties in the Federalists and Anti-Federalists laid the foundation for two parties based on two distinct sets of interests. See figure 9-3, p. 275 for a look at sectional politics. Political socialization of children to identify with the party of the parent has been an important factor in maintaining the two-party system, which was already established. The political culture has been one of consensus, and moderation. This has helped to maintain the two-party system. The winner-take-all election system, particularly the Electoral College for electing the President, makes it very difficult for third parties to have any electoral success. Finally, most state and federal election laws provide a clear advantage to the two major parties. Third party candidates for President are not eligible for federal matching funds.[p. 274-278]

The Role of Minor Parties in U.S. Political History

Minor parties have not been able to compete very successfully with the two major parties, but have played an important role in our political life. Ideological based minor parties, such as the Socialist Party, remain active today, and had real electoral success in the early twentieth century. The most successful minor parties split from the major parties. The Bull Moose Progressive Party in 1912 nominated Theodore Roosevelt for President, which created a three-way race, and gave the election to the Democrat Woodrow Wilson. A Democrat splinter party, the American Independent Party, supported George Wallace for President in 1968, and he did receive 46 electoral votes for President, but this did not seem to affect the outcome of Richard Nixon's victory. Other minor parties, which include the Greenback and Populists, have appeared for specific economic issues, and then fairly quickly disappeared. Minor parties have had an impact on American politics by raising important political issues, which are usually taken over by the two major parties, and in some cases determining the outcome of the presidential election. The third party candidate in 1992, H. Ross Perot, probably took votes away from Republican George Bush to give the victory to Democrat Bill Clinton. [p. 279-281].

The Uncertain Future of Party Identification

The current state of political party identification seems to indicate a movement away from the two major parties. Thirty Four percent of voters today classify themselves as independents. See Figure 9-4 page 282.

Political Parties and Representative Government

When the party elects its members to hold government office, there are a number of factors, which limit the ability of the party to carry out its programs. The American check and balance system works to control parties because the voting public seems to prefer a "divided government" with the executive and legislative branches controlled by different parties. This is evident in the increasing trend of ticket splitting. There is also a lack of cohesion in American parties, which means that you cannot count on every elected party official to support the programs of the party. [p. 282-285]

Political Parties: Why Are They Important Today?

American political parties face a number of challenges for the future. Parties must address the issues of what they offer to the voters, what to do about independent candidates that can fund their own campaign or form their own political party, and the dilemma of, do the major parties actually stand for different positions on the issues? [p. 285].

KEY TERMS

Divided government - p. 261
Electoral College - p. 277
Era of personal politics - p. 264
Faction - p. 261
Independent - p. 261
National committee - p. 270
National convention - p. 268
Party platform - p. 268

Patronage - p. 271
Political party - p. 261
Splinter party - p. 279
Third party - p. 279
Ticket-splitting - p. 272
Two-party system - p. 262
Unit rule - p. 271

OTHER RESOURCES

A number of valuable supplements are available to students using the Schmidt, Shelley, and Bardes text. The full list of the supplements is in the preface to this study guide. Ask your instructor how to obtain these resources. One supplement is highlighted here, the INFOTRAC Online Library.

INFOTRAC EXERCISES

Log on to http://www.infotrac-college.com.
Enter your Pass code that came with your textbook.
You can access the article by typing the exact phrase below.

Patronage
Continuing Judicial Assault Patronage
The premise of this article is the Supreme Court of the U.S. has continued the assault on patronage practices in the state of Illinois. Chicago is the first major city under a court-approved monitoring program to ensure the end of political patronage.

Study Questions
1. Why are the cases against patronage centered in Illinois?
2. What are some of the problems trying to eliminate patronage?

PRACTICE EXAM
(Answers appear at the end of this chapter.)

Fill-in-the-Blank. Supply the missing word(s) or term to complete the sentence.

1. A _____ _____ is a group of individuals who organize to win elections, to operate the government, and to determine public policy.

2. The first _____ political division in the United States occurred prior to the adoption of the Constitution.

3. The _____ Party is the oldest continuing political party in the western world.

4. The major political American political party, which emerged in the late 1850s from the remains of the Whig Party, was the _____ _____.

5. Each layer in the formal structure of a political party is virtually _____ from the other layers.

6. The real strength and power of a national party is at the _____ level.

7. The national chairperson of the party is selected during the _____ _____.

8. The period from the Civil War to the 1920s has been called one of _____ _____.

9. The Democrat party has been known in modern times at the party of _____ and _____ classes and _____ groups.

10. Most minor parties that have endured have had a strong _____ foundation.

True/False   Circle the appropriate letter to indicate if the statement is true or false.

T   F   1.   Party-in-the-Electorate is those members of the general public, who express a preference for one party over another.

T   F   2.   American political parties are tightly organized pyramid-shaped organizations with the national chairperson dictating policy to lower levels.

T   F   3.   The party platform is largely ignored once one of the two major parties captures control of the government.

T   F   4.   The national chairperson for the two major parties is actually chosen by their respective party's presidential nominee.

T   F   5.   The Federal Election Commission (FEC) rules for campaign financing place restrictions on minor party candidates.

T   F   6.   In terms of foreign policy, the general public feels the Democratic Party does a better job than the Republican Party.

T   F   7.   Virtually all levels of government in the United States use the plurality, winner-take-all electoral system.

T   F   8.   The Green Party may have had an impact on the 2000 presidential election.

T   F   9.   Minor parties have not played an important role in American politics.

T   F   10. It appears that the electorate is increasingly voting a straight ticket.

Multiple Choice Circle the correct response.

1.   The main feature differentiating a faction from a political party is that a faction
     a.   is composed only of conservatives, while a political party may have both liberals and conservatives
     b.   generally does not have a permanent organized structure
     c.   works best if there are competing factions in opposition to it
     d.   helps to extend democracy to the rank-and-file party member.

2.   Political parties in the United States tend to perform all of the following activities except
     a.   recruit candidates for public office
     b.   organize and run elections
     c.   act as the organized opposition to the party in power
     d.   establish a large cadre of highly disciplined dues-paying party members

3.   The first two opposing groups in United States politics were the
     a.   Democrats and Republicans
     b.   Federalists and Anti-Federalists
     c.   Washingtonians and Jeffersonians
     d.   Independents and Whigs

4. The era from 1816 to 1828 when attention was centered on the character of the individual running for office rather than on party identification is referred to as
    a. the era of good feeling
    b. factional politics
    c. personal politics
    d. democratic politics

5. After the end of the Civil, the _____ became heavily Democratic, and the _____ became heavily Republican.
    a. North-South
    b. South-North
    c. East-West
    d. West-East

6. The modern party system was created from the
    a. Post-Civil War period
    b. Progressive Movement
    c. New Deal period
    d. Vietnam protest period

7. The main purpose of the national party conventions every four years is to
    a. nominate the presidential and vice-presidential candidates
    b. write a party platform
    c. check the credentials of all party activists
    d. develop a strategy for the upcoming presidential election.

8. In terms of party organization, the real strength and power of the Democratic and Republican parties
    a. resides with their members in the U.S. Congress
    b. is determined by their national committee chairpersons
    c. resides at the state level of party organization
    d. is determined by the number of election victories each party has in a given time period

9. The principal organized structure within states for each political party is the
    a. precinct committee
    b. ward captain
    c. state central committee
    d. governor's council

10. Rewarding members of a political party with government jobs and/or contracts is known as
    a. bribery
    b. graft and corruption
    c. non-competitive bidding
    d. patronage

11. Since the presidency of Franklin D. Roosevelt, the core of the Democratic Party has been
    a. middle-class, working Americans
    b. upper-class liberals
    c. minorities, the working class and ethnic groups
    d. middle to upper-class protestants and independents

12. The pursuit of political interest interests which are of special concern to a region or section of the country is
    a. sectional politics
    b. special politics
    c. dirty politics
    d. federal politics

13. The major division in American politics has been over _____ issues.
    a. religious
    b. social
    c. foreign policy
    d. economic

14. The most successful minor parties have been those that have
    a. focused on the positive things in life, not the negative
    b. been formed from the break-up of the Democratic party prior to WWI
    c. split from major parties
    d. opposed the existing economic power structure

15. Which of the following statement about party identification is true?
    a. In recent years, Democrats have increased, while Republicans and Independents have decreased
    b. In recent years, Independents have increased, while Democrats and Republicans have decreased
    c. In recent years, Republicans have increased, while Democrats and Independents have decreased
    d. In recent years, Democrats, Republicans, and Independents have decreased

16. The most important reason for the creation of splinter parties is
    a. ideology
    b. class politics
    c. a particular political personality
    d. the U.S. political culture

17. The third party which may have cost Democrat Al Gore the presidency in the 2000 election was
    a. Green Party
    b. Reform Party
    c. Socialist Party
    d. Libertarian Party

18. Independent voters in the 2000 presidential election, composed _____ percent of the electorate.
    a. 34
    b. 40
    c. 50
    d. 55

19. Calling the U.S., a two-party system is an oversimplification because
    a. a third party candidate almost won the 2000 presidential election
    b. the nature and names of the two major parties have changed over time
    c. ideology is such an important factor in U.S. elections
    d. third parties receive equal public funding with major parties

20. The best indication that political parties have weakened in the last three decades is
    a. low voter turnout
    b. low party identification
    c. high numbers of PACs
    d. the lack of media coverage

Short Essay Questions   Briefly address the major concepts raised by the following questions.

1. Distinguish between a political party, interest group and faction.

2. Trace the evolution of political party development within the United States.

3. Identify the formal structure of political party organization in America.

4. Discuss the reasons for the two-party system in the United States.

ANSWERS TO THE PRACTICE EXAM

Fill-in-the-blank

1. political party   [p. 261]
2. partisan   [p. 263]
3. Democratic   [p. 265]
4. Republican Party   [p. 265]
5. autonomous   [p. 268]
6. state   [p. 270]
7. national convention   [p. 270]
8. sectional politics   [p. 275]
9. minorities, working, ethnic [p. 276]
10. ideological   [p. 279]

True/False

| 1. | T | [p. 267] | 3. | F | [p. 268] | 5. | T | [p. 277] | 7. | T | [p. 276] | 9. | F | [p. 281] |
| 2. | F | [p. 268] | 4. | T | [p. 270] | 6. | F | [p. 273] | 8. | T | [p. 281] | 10. | F | [p. 282] |

Multiple Choice.

1.	b	[p. 261]	6.	c	[p. 266]	11.	c	[p. 273]	16.	c	[p. 279]
2.	d	[p. 262]	7.	a	[p. 268]	12.	a	[p. 275]	17.	a	[p. 281]
3.	b	[p. 263]	8.	c	[p. 271]	13.	d	[p. 276]	18.	a	[p. 282]
4.	c	[p. 264]	9.	c	[p. 271]	14.	c	[p. 279]	19.	b	[p. 281]
5.	b	[p. 265]	10.	d	[p. 271]	15.	b	[p. 282]	20.	b	[p. 282]

Short Essay Questions   Briefly address the major concepts raised by the following questions.

1. Distinguish between a political party, interest group and faction. [p. 261]

    •   A political party is a group of political activists who organize to win elections, to operate the government, and to determine public policy.
    •   An interest group is a collection of individuals that attempt to influence elections, influence the elected officials, and to influence public policy.
    •   Factions are smaller groups, which may exist within political parties, and are trying to obtain certain benefits for themselves.

2. Trace the evolution of political party development within the United States. [p. 262-267]

    - The formation of political parties in the U.S. went through six basic periods. These are; (1) the creation of parties, (2) the era of personal politics, (3) the period of President Jackson to the Civil War, (4), the post-Civil War period, (5) the progressive period, and (6) the modern period.
        - The first parties were created from 1789 to 1812 around support for ratifying the Constitution, the Federalists or against ratification, the Anti-Federalists.
        - From 1816 to 1828, voters focused on the candidates rather than the parties.
        - From 1828 to 1860, political parties tended to focus on Andrew Jackson, and the Democratic and Whig parties developed.
        - The post-Civil War period of 1864 to 1892 created our current two-party system, as the anti-slavery Republican Party was created.
        - The Progressive era from 1896 to 1928 led to the split in the Republican Party, and the election of the Democrats in 1912, which enacting much of the Progressive Party platform.
        - The New Deal programs of President Franklin Roosevelt, which established the current political landscape of the political party system, created the modern period from 1932.

3. Identify the formal structure of political party organization in America. [p. 268-272].

    - The formal political party organization structure consists of the national level, the state level and the local level. See the theoretical structure of political parties, Figure 9-2 page 282.
        - The national party organization consists of a national convention, held every four years. At this convention, the party selects its candidates for president and vice president, writes a party platform, selects a national committee, and selects a national chairperson.
        - The state central committee will carry out the decisions of the state party convention, and in some states direct the activities of the state chairperson.
        - The local party organization called the grass roots uses county committees, and their chairperson to direct and assist the activities of precinct leaders.

4. Discuss the reasons for the two-party system in the United States. [p. 274-278]
    - The historical foundations of the two-party system developed around relatively district sets of issues.
    - The first of these issues were ratifying the Constitution, which led to the Federalists and Anti-Federalists.
    - Political socialization in which parents influence the children choice of political party continued the two-party system.
    - The American political culture emphasizes the commonality of goals, which make the two party board, and able to accommodate different viewpoints.
    - The winner-take-all election system makes it very difficult for third parties to win elections.
    - State and federal election laws make it difficult for third parties to get on the ballot.

Chapter 10
CAMPAIGNS, NOMINATIONS, AND ELECTIONS

CHAPTER SUMMARY

The People Who Run for Political Office

People who run for political office can be divided into two groups; those who are "self-starters, and those who are recruited. [p. 294]. There are few constitutional requirements to run for federal office. For President, a candidate must be a natural-born citizen, age 35, and a resident of the U.S for fourteen years, when sworn in. For Vice President, the same requirements as President, and cannot be a resident of the same state as the President. For Senator, a citizen for nine years, 30 years old, and a resident of the state elected from. For Representative, a citizen for seven years, 25 years old, and a resident of the state elected from. [p. 295] While these requirements are minimal, most current office holders are white males. This is largely because of past discrimination, and women for one group, have made tremendous gains in elected officials in the last 10 years. See Figure 10-1 page 296, for a look at the number of women candidates, and representatives elected. Most candidates elected to office tend to be professionals, especially lawyers. [p. 296-297]

The Modern Campaign Machine

American political campaigns are extravagant yearlong events that cost a total of several billion dollars in 1998. As was noted in chapter 9, fewer people are identifying with political parties now, which means that campaigns are changing and candidates have to spend more money to get out the vote with paid staff. Most candidates, since the 1960s, will hire a professional paid political consultant to run the campaign. [p. 297-298].

The Strategy of Winning

The goal of every political campaign is to win the election. One of the most important concerns is how known the candidate is. The problem of name recognition is obviously a problem for a third party candidate, because they do not have the well-known Democrat or Republican name to run on. Most candidates will use two major strategies in the campaign, polls, and focus groups. Polls give the candidate information, and as the election approaches, tracking polls indicate how well the campaign is going. Focus groups allow the candidate to gain insights into the public's perception of the candidate. [p. 298-299]

Financing the Campaign

The tremendous cost of political campaigns has caused a lot of concern among the public and led Congress to pass a number of laws to attempt to regulate campaign financing. Beginning in 1925, the Corrupt Practices Acts were passed, but proved largely ineffective. The Hatch Act in 1939 attempted to limit spending by political groups, but was also easily evaded. The Federal Election Campaign Act of 1972 and 1974 essentially replaced all past laws and instituted a major reform. These laws created the Federal Election Commission (FEC), provided public funding for presidential elections, put limits on presidential spending, limited campaign contributions, and required disclosure by candidates. Within a few years of these laws, three major loopholes appeared. Soft money, given to political parties, independent expenditures, is money to help a candidate, but not part of his campaign, and bundling, adding together maximum contributions to influence a candidate, were all used to evade the new campaign financing laws. The Bipartisan Campaign Reform Act of 2002 bans soft money. How effective this law will be, remains to be seen. [p. 299-304]

Running for President: The Longest Campaign

The American presidential election has two distinct phases. The first begins in January with the first presidential primary and end in June with the party's national convention. The second phase usually begins on Labor Day, and culminated in the presidential election in November. After the riots at the 1968 Democratic National Convention, caused major changes in the primary election system, presidential candidates realized that the primary elections could be a springboard to win the presidency. If a candidate wins the first caucus in Iowa, and the first primary in New Hampshire, they will be labeled a front-runner by the media, and receive a big boost in their campaign. Other states, attempting to get the media coverage, and influence in the presidential nomination, began to move up the day of their primary elections.

A number of southern states moved their primaries to the same day, which became known as Super Tuesday. This practice of moving up the date of a presidential primary is known as front-loading. The national convention is the end result of all the state primary elections. In recent years, the delegates selected in the primaries have already given the nomination to a candidate before the convention begins. This has lessened the interest and media coverage of the national convention. [p. 304-308]

The Electoral College

The Constitution has created the Electoral College as the official method for electing the President. Each state is responsible for selecting electors, who will officially vote for president. These electors are based on the number of Senators and Representatives that a state has. The total number of electors is 538. See Figure 10-2, Page 308 for each states electoral votes. If a plurality of voters in a state chooses one slate of electors, then those electors are pledged to vote on the first Monday after the second Wednesday in December in the state capital for the president and vice president. The ballots are counted and certified before a joint session of Congress early in January. It requires 270 electoral votes to be elected president. See Figure 10-3, page 309 for a view of the overall process. This process has been criticized for a number of reasons, including the possibility that a candidate could win the popular vote, but lose the electoral vote. Th states with small electoral votes are ignored in the presidential campaign, but do get more electoral votes for fewer people. The major reforms of the system, which have been suggested, are to have direct election of the president, and to require electors to vote for the candidate that has a plurality in the state. [p .308-311].

How Are Elections Conducted?

The United States uses the secret or Australian ballot for elections, which is prepared, distributed, and counted by government officials at public expense. There are two types of ballots, the office-block, which focuses on the office rather than the party, and the party-column, which focuses on the party rather than the office. In recent years, registering and voting have been available through the mail. Experts are divided over whether voting by mail increases participation or only increase the opportunity for fraud. [p. 311-314].

Voting in National, State, and Local Elections

Voting turnout in the United States in the 2000 presidential election was only 50.7 percent of eligible voters. There are two theories about the decline of voting turnout in the U.S. One is that the decline in voting turnout is a threat to our democracy. The other is that people are basically satisfied with the status quo, and that is why they don't vote. Studies show that there are a number of factors, which seem to influence voting turnout. These factors are age, education, minority status, income, and two-party competition. Voters tend to be older, more educated, not minorities, wealthy, and where there is two-party competition. See Table 10-3, p. 316 and figure 10-4, p. 315 for a look at different turnout rates. Political scientists believe that people don't vote because of a political withdrawal since 1960, and the rational ignorance effect, in which people chose not find out about issues because they believe their vote will not make a difference. See Tables 10-4, 10-5 for types of voting, p. 317. [p. 314-318]

Legal Restrictions on Voting

Historically only white males who owned property were allowed to vote. The Constitution allowed the states to decide who should vote. Since the Civil War, Constitutional Amendments, and act of Congress, such as the Voting Rights Act, have extended the right to vote. Voting requires registration, and some scholars believe that even the minimal requirements of citizenship, age and residency, keep some people from voting. [p. 318-319].

How Do Voters Decide?

The factors that influence voting decisions seem to be socioeconomic and demographic factors and psychological factors. Socioeconomic and demographic factors include education, income and socioeconomic status, religion, ethnic background, gender, age, and geographic region. See Table 10-6 page 320 for a view of how these factors influence voting in selected presidential election years. A discussion of these factors continues to page 325. Psychological factors include party identification, the image or perception of the candidate, and issues, particularly economic issues. See Table 10-7, p. 322 about Labor voters. [p. 319-325]

Campaigns, Nominations, and Elections: Why Are They Important Today?
The length and cost of political campaigns will continue to be issues of concern. The most pressing issue for the future seems to be the increasingly level of cynicism of voters, which may be a major factor in the low levels of participation at all governmental elections. [p. 325].

KEY TERMS

Australian ballot - p. 311
Caucus - p. 305
Corrupt Practices Act - p. 300
Elector - p. 308
Front-loading - p. 307
Hatch Act - p. 300
Independent expenditures - p. 303
Office-block ballot - p. 311

Party-column ballot - p.311
Presidential primary - p. 294
Rational ignorance effect - p. 318
Socioeconomic status - p. 320
Soft money - p. 303
Tracking polls - p. 299
Voting turnout - p. 314

OTHER RESOURCES

A number of valuable supplements are available to students using the Schmidt, Shelley, and Bardes text. The full list of the supplements is in the preface to this study guide. Ask your instructor how to obtain these resources. One supplement is highlighted here, the INFOTRAC Online Library.

INFOTRAC EXERCISES

Log on to http://www.infotrac-college.com.
Enter your Pass code that came with your textbook.
Use the CD that came with your textbook for suggestions for articles in this chapter.

PRACTICE EXAM
(Answers appear at the end of this chapter.)

Fill-in-the-Blank. Supply the missing word(s) or term to complete the sentence.

1. In terms of characteristics, holders of political office in the U.S. are overwhelmingly _____ and _____.

2. Candidates who run for office are described as "self-starters", and _____.

3. In the last three decades, campaigns have changed from volunteer campaign managers to paid _____ _____.

4. Campaign contributions banned by the Bipartisan Campaign Act of 2002 are referred to as _____ _____.

5. Today, candidates use focus groups, and _____ _____ to find out how the campaign is going.

6. Each state's number of electors in the Electoral College equals to the state's number of _____ plus its number of _____ in the U.S. Congress.

7. A _____ _____ is a form of general election ballot in which the candidates are arranged in one column under their respective party name and symbol.

8.   Citizenship, age and _____ are key requirements to register to vote.

9.   The higher the income, the more likely a person is to vote for the _____ Party.

10. With the possible exception of race, _____ _____ has been the most important determinant of voting in national elections.

True/False   Circle the appropriate letter to indicate if the statement is true or false.

T   F   1.   Today, when campaigning for public office, candidates are depending more and more upon the resources of political parties.

T   F   2.   Political campaigns seem to be getting longer and more excessive each year.

T   F   3.   Tracking polls are used by the government to keep track of campaign contributions.

T   F   4.   The purpose of instituting the primary election was to open the nomination process to ordinary party members.

T   F   5.   States began to change the dates of primaries to have more influence in nominating. presidential candidates in a process known as, front-loading.

T   F   6.   The framers of the constitution favored the selection of the president and vice president by the masses.

T   F   7.   In general, the more education you have the more likely you are to vote.

T   F   8.   Public funding of political campaigns is provided by law for all national elections.

T   F   9.   Today, all states have uniform qualifications for voting and registration requirements.

T   F   10. Historically, economic issues have the strongest influence on voter's choices.

Multiple Choice   Circle the correct response.

1.   The constitutional qualifications for the office of president include all of the following EXCEPT
     a.   natural born citizen
     b.   35 years of age
     c.   14-year resident of U.S.
     d.   registered voter.

2.   Which of the following characteristics is <u>not</u> descriptive of a professional campaign?
     a.   Increased length of campaign.
     b.   Paid political consultant.
     c.   Increased costs of campaign.
     d.   Increased use of volunteers.

3.   The first attempt by Congress to regulate campaign spending was the
     a.   Hatch Act
     b.   Corrupt Practices Acts
     c.   CREEP Act
     d.   Federal Election Campaign Act

4. The purpose of the Federal Election Commission is to
   a. create an aura of good feeling in federal elections.
   b. Oversee and enforce the provisions of the 1974 Federal Election Campaign Act.
   c. Scrutinize and attempt to discover loopholes in the 1974 Act
   d. Oversee federal and state elections.

5. The group that now controls the nomination process for president is the
   a. mass public
   b. party elites
   c. presidential nominees, themselves
   d. mass media

6. The framers of the constitution established the Electoral College because they wanted
   a. to ensure the general population would have an opportunity to directly vote for president.
   b. the choice of president and vice-president to be made by a few dispassionate, reasonable men.
   c. only candidates for president and vice-president who had graduated from the Electoral College.
   d. the political parties to be able to control the selection of president and vice-president.

7. The major parties are not in favor of eliminating the Electoral College because
   a. the electors are always influential party members, who might be offended.
   b. the major party candidates would not receive as much public funding
   c. the masses are not capable of making this important decision
   d. they fear it would give minor parties a more influential role in the election outcome.

8. The form of ballot that encourages straight-ticket voting is the
   a. closed ballot
   b. open ballot
   c. office-block ballot
   d. party-column ballot

9. The coattail effect
   a. is only in national elections.
   b. refers to voting by mail.
   c. is the influence of the candidate that is at the top of the ballot.
   d. is an aspect of voter fraud.

10. Which statement is correct with respect to age as a factor in voting?
    a. Age is not a significant factor in voting.
    b. Younger voters tend to turn out in higher percentages than older voters.
    c. Turnout increases the older the age groups until the age of 65 and older.
    d. Younger voters have more enthusiasm for voting than older voters.

11. As a factor in voting, more education seems to be correlated with
    a. voting Republican
    b. voting Democratic
    c. voting independent
    d. disillusionment and apathy

12. Since their introduction in the late nineteenth century, voter registration laws have
    a. increased the numbers of voters.
    b. reduced the voting of African Americans and immigrants.
    c. created a new class of active and committed voters
    d. allowed the manipulation of election results by party bosses.

13. If we measure the influence of socioeconomic status by profession, then
    a. skilled tradesman tend to vote independently.
    b. unskilled workers tend to vote more than skilled workers do.
    c. those of higher socioeconomic status tend to vote Republican.
    d. those of higher socioeconomic status tend to vote Democratic.

14. With the possible exception of race, the most important determinant of voting behavior in national elections is
    a. religion
    b. age
    c. party identification
    d. income

15. Historically, the issues that have the strongest influence on voters' choice have been
    a. religious
    b. foreign policy issues
    c. environmental issues
    d. economic issues

16. Which of the following is a provision of the Bipartisan Campaign Reform Act of 2002?
    a. bans all soft-money contributions
    b. bans all outside special interest ads
    c. limits individual contributions to $1,000 per individual
    d. bans only soft-money contribution to national political parties

17. Front-Loading of presidential primaries refers to the practice of
    a. spending massive sums of money on the first primary
    b. being the first candidate to announce a campaign for the presidency
    c. moving presidential primary elections to the early part of the campaign
    d. using the national convention to select the candidate

18. Norman Ornstein criticizes mail-in voting because
    a. it leads to massive fraud
    b. it will lead to Internet voting
    c. the mail is often late
    d. it subverts the whole process by mail in voters casting an uninformed vote

19. Which of the following measures to improve voter turnout have not been tried?
    a. mail-in voting
    b. registering when you apply for a driver's license
    c. absentee voting
    d. declaring election day a national holiday

20. Issue voting in the early 2000s was
    a. very important
    b. moderately important
    c. less important
    d. not a factor at all

Short Essay Questions   Briefly address the major concepts raised by the following questions.

1.   Describe the presidential election process from primaries to the general election.

2.   Explain the legislative action taken to try to reform campaign financing.

3.   Describe and explain the factors associated with voting.

4.   Discuss the Electoral College procedures and proposed reforms.

ANSWERS TO THE PRACTICE EXAM

Fill-in-the-blank

1.	white, male	[p. 296]
2.	recruited	[p. 294]
3.	Political Consultant	[p. 298]
4.	soft money	[p. 303]
5.	tracking polls	[p. 299]
6.	senators, representatives	[p. 308]
7.	party-column	[p. 311]
8.	residency	[p. 319]
9.	Republican	[p. 322]
10.	party identification	[p. 324]

True/False

1.	F	[p. 297]	3.	F	[p. 299]	5.	T	[p. 306]	7.	T	[p. 316]
2.	T	[p. 297]	4.	T	[p. 304]	6.	F	[p. 308]	8.	F	[p. 300]

9.   F   [p. 319]
10. T   [p. 325]

Multiple Choice.

1.	d	[p. 295]	6.	b	[p. 308]	11.	a	[p. 321]	16.	d	[p. 304]
2.	d	[p. 298]	7.	d	[p. 311]	12.	b	[p. 319]	17.	c	[p. 306]
3.	b	[p. 300]	8.	d	[p. 311]	13.	c	[p. 320]	18.	d	[p. 312]
4.	b	[p. 300]	9.	c	[p. 311]	14.	c	[p. 324]	19.	d	[p. 318]
5.	a	[p. 304]	10.	c	[p. 316]	15.	d	[p. 325]	20.	c	[p. 325]

Short Essay Questions   Briefly address the major concepts raised by the following questions.

1.   Explain the legislative action taken to try to reform campaign financing. [p. 299-304].

- Congress in 1925 passed a series of acts called the Corrupt Practices Acts, which were largely ineffective.
- The Hatch Act passed in 1939 put limits on the amount of money that political groups could contribute to political campaigns.
- The Federal Election Campaign Act of 1972 replaced the past laws and instituted a major reform.
- After the Watergate scandal, the Federal election Campaign Act of 1974 created more reform. It did the following.
  - Created the Federal Election Commission.
  - Provided public funding for presidential primaries and general elections.
  - Limited presidential campaign spending.
  - Limited contributions
  - Required disclosure.
- 1976 Amendments to the law allowed for the creation of Political Action Committees.
- Bipartisan Campaign Reform Act of 2002 prohibited soft money in federal elections.

2. Describe the presidential election process from primaries to the general election. [p. 304-308].

   - The presidential process is two different campaigns from January to November linked together by the political party's national conventions.
     - The presidential primary system begins with the Iowa caucus in January and New Hampshire primary in February. The winner of these elections is dubbed the front-runner by the media, which gives that candidate a big boost in their campaign.
     - States have moved their primary dates in recent years to try to have more influence in the nomination of presidential candidates. California has moved its primary to March, in a process, which is known as front-loading. Southern states hold their primaries on the same date, known as Super Tuesday.
     - The caucuses and primaries select delegates, who go to the national convention. The main purpose of the national convention is to nominate the president and vice-president.
     - The president and vice-president begin the campaign to capture the office in the general election around Labor Day.

3. Discuss the Electoral College procedures and proposed reforms. [p. 308-311].

   - The Electoral College is the constitutionally required method for the selection of the president and vice-president.
   - Each state's electors are selected during the presidential election year. Each stares has the number of electors equal to that state's number of senators (two) plus it number of representatives. See Figure 10-2, page 325 for the number of electors for each state.
   - The slate of electors in a state is elected by the candidate, which has a plurality vote. In other words, the most votes of any candidate. See Figure 10-3, for the process of the Electoral College vote. It takes 270 electoral votes to win the presidency.
   - The two major suggested reforms of the Electoral College are to elect the president by popular vote, and require each elector by law to vote for the candidate that received the plurality.

4. Describe and explain the factors associated with voting. [p. 316-318]

   - There is an established relationship between voting participation and the following factors: age, educational attainment, minority status, income level, and the existence of two-party competition.
     - Young people vote in the lowest percentages. The voting turnout increased with each age group until 65 years and over. See Table 10-3, page 316.
     - The more education a person has, the more likely they are to vote. The voting turnout increases with each level of education until college graduation. See Table 10-4, page 317.
     - Wealthier people tend to vote in higher numbers. People with annual family incomes of $50, 000 or more, are twice as likely to vote as people with annual family incomes of under $15, 000.
     - States, which have competitive two party elections, have higher turnout rates.

Chapter 11
THE MEDIA AND CYBERPOLITICS

CHAPTER SUMMARY

The Media's Functions
The mass media performs six functions in U.S. society. These functions are: (1) entertainment, (2) reporting the news, (3) identifying public problems, (4) socializing new generations, (5) providing a political forum, and (6) making profits. Entertainment has the greatest media time devoted to it, and sometimes stimulates discussion of important issues presented in drama form. Reporting the news is a primary media function in a democracy. The media is crucial in identifying problems, and helping to set the public agenda. The content of media, particularly television, offers children and immigrants a view of the basic American values. The political forum feature allows citizens a way to participate in the public debate. Finally, media is privately own for profit. This makes for a complex relationship and balance for public opinion, government, and the media. [p. 333-335].

History of the Media in the United States
The earliest media in the United States was the newspaper. Some historians feel that the printed media played an important role in unifying the country. Many of these early newspapers were politically sponsored. In the nineteenth century, the high-speed rotary press, and the telegraph led to the creation of mass-readership newspapers. The late nineteenth century saw sensationalistic, irresponsible journalism among these newspapers, which was called yellow journalism. In 1920, the first scheduled radio broadcast transmitted the returns of 1920 presidential election. This was the beginning of broadcast media, radio and television. Today, cable, satellite television, and the Internet have created narrow casting, which allows the electronic media to target small sectors of the audience. Another recent development has been the rise of literally thousands of talk shows on radio, television, and Internet. [p. 335-341].

The Primacy of Television
Television is the most influential medium. The use of images conveys powerful content. The format of television tends to produce brief memorable comments called sound bites, which can be easily fitted into the news broadcast. These sound bites have perhaps increased the impact of television on political events. [p. 341].

The Media and Political Campaigns
Advertising for political candidates is one of the most influential uses of mass media. Perhaps the most effective political ads of all time, was the "Daisy Girl" ad, used by President Johnson against Barry Goldwater in the 1968 presidential election. Since this advertisement, the concept of negative advertising has come to be a major part of many political campaigns. Political advertising is the most expensive part of the political campaign, so candidates have attempted to use free coverage by the news media for their advantage. Political campaign advisers, called spin-doctors, attempt to interpret campaign event news in a positive way for the candidate. This is referred to as putting spin on a story or event. Televised presidential debates have become a feature of the presidential elections, since the 1960 debate between John Kennedy and Richard Nixon. Candidates soon realized that the image that they presented on television was a critical aspect of any political campaign. The question of how much influence all this media coverage has on voters is hard to answer, because of the many factors that influence how someone votes. Studies do tend to indicate that media seems to have the biggest impact on voters who are truly undecided on whom to vote for. [p. 342-346].

The Media and the Government

The mass media not only has a big influence on political campaigns, but it also has influence on government and government officials. The president has a love-hate relationship with the media. The White House press corps attempt to find out news about the president, and the president's press secretary tries to just give the press corps, the information that the president wants them to have. The media and the president need each other to survive. Perhaps no president was as successful at using the media, than Franklin D. Roosevelt, who brought a new spirit to a demoralized country during the Great Depression. The media also plays a very big role in setting the public agenda. Although the media does not decide the agenda, they do raise up certain issues to be decided upon. [p. 346-347].

Government Regulation of the Media

Although the United States has the freest press in the world, regulation of media does exist. Electronic media, who did not exist when the constitution was written, has been regulated more than print medium. The Federal Communication Commission (FCC) was created to regulate broadcast media. In the 1996 Telecommunications Act, Congress opened up the telephone, television, and Internet industries to vast mergers. The question for the future is how to prevent the giant telecommunication companies of today, from becoming giant monopolies. In general, the broadcasting industry has avoided government regulation of content by establishing it own code. There has been increasing debate about banning the broadcast of polls, and early predications of winners in presidential elections. This "early calling" of elections has seemed to have had some impact on the outcome of voting. The Telecommunication Act of 1996 had two provisions to control content of media. One provision required television manufacturers to put a "V-chip" in each set to allow parents to block television programs. The other provision attempted to regulate content on the Internet. The Supreme Court ruled this provision unconstitutional in 1997. [p.347-348].

The Public's Right to Media Access

Both the Federal Communication Commission and the courts have supported the concept that citizens have a right of access to media. The airwaves are public, and the government can dictate to the private companies how to use these airwaves. Technology in the form of the Internet is giving citizens more and more access. [p. 348-349.]

Bias in the Media

Many studies have attempted to determine if there is some clearly recognized bias in media. For years, it was assumed that there was a bias toward the liberal ideology. In recent years, the bias seems to have slipped more to the conservative ideology. Thomas Patterson's view from his recent book is that the bias of media is to emphasize bad news and cynicism rather than any political position. [p. 349-351].

The Media: Why Are They Important Today?

The Internet in 1999 has created literally thousands of sites to allow citizens to "chat" with each other, journalists, and politicians. The intensity of these conversations seems to indicate that Americans to eager to use this new technology to invigorate our democracy. [p. 351].

KEY TERMS

Bias - p. 349
electronic media - p. 339
managed news - p. 336
media access - p. 348
narrow casting - p. 340
press secretary - p. 346

public agenda - p. 335
sound bite - p. 341
spin - p. 343
spin doctor - p. 343
White House press corps - p. 346
Yellow journalism - p. 338

OTHER RESOURCES

A number of valuable supplements are available to students using the Schmidt, Shelley, and Bardes text. The full list of the supplements is in the preface to this study guide. Ask your instructor how to obtain these resources. One supplement is highlighted here, the INFOTRAC Online Library.

INFOTRAC EXERCISES

Log on to http://www.infotrac-college.com.
Enter your Pass code that came with your textbook.
Use the CD that came with your textbook for suggestions for articles in this chapter.

PRACTICE EXAM
(Answers appear at the end of this chapter.)

Fill-in-the-Blank. Supply the missing word(s) or term to complete the sentence.

1. By far, the greatest number of radio and television hours is dedicated to _____ _____ _____.

2. The mass media in all their forms have as their primary goals the _____ _____ _____.

3. A term for sensationalistic, irresponsible journalism is _____ _____.

4. Specialized programming by the media for specialized tastes is referred to as _____ _____.

5. _____ is the most influential of the media.

6. In television news coverage, a several-second comment selected or crated for its immediate impact is referred to as a _____ _____.

7. An interpretation of campaign events or election results that is most favorable to a candidate's campaign strategy is referred to as the _____.

8. The individual responsible for representing the White House before the media is the _____ _____.

9. The government has much greater control over the_____ media than it does over the _____ media.

10. The FCC and the courts have ruled that _____ have a right of access to media.

True/False Circle the appropriate letter to indicate if the statement is true or false.

T   F   1. Thomas Jefferson was a firm believer in control of the press by government.

T   F   2. Many historians believe that the growth if the print media played an important role in unifying the country.

T   F   3. The effect of more diversified cable television broadcasting has been to make television more and more like print media with specialized tastes.

T	F	4.	Newspapers are today the primary news source for the majority of Americans.
T	F	5.	In general, challengers have much more to gain from debating than do incumbents.
T	F	6.	It appears that the media are most influential with those who have not formed an opinion about political candidates or issues.
T	F	7.	Studies indicate that the media is not playing an important role today in setting the public agenda.
T	F	8.	The United States has the most highly regulated press in the world
T	F	9.	The government places fewer restrictions on the broadcast media than it places on the print media.
T	F	10.	The government has a right to dictate how the airwaves are used because the airwaves are public domain, used for private profit.

Multiple Choice Circle the correct response.

1. By far the greatest number of radio and television broadcast hours are dedicated to
   a. news analysis
   b. sport broadcasting
   c. entertaining the public
   d. educational programming

2. Information generated and distributed by the government in such a way as to give government interests priority over the facts is referred to as
   a. fairness doctrine
   b. right-to-know rule
   c. narrow casting
   d. managed news

3. The type of media which has increased the largest percentage in the last fifteen years is
   a. cable
   b. network affiliates
   c. PBS
   d. independent stations

4. The 1960 presidential campaign was the first to involve the use of
   a. political action committees
   b. presidential preference primaries
   c. radio in a meaningful way
   d. televised presidential debates

5. The term narrow casting refers to
   a. presenting only one side of an issue
   b. media programming for specialized tastes
   c. a biased news report
   d. presenting a narrow image to your readership

6. The first network broadcast of electronic media was in the
    a. 1920s
    b. 1930s
    c. 1940s
    d. 1950s

7. Negative advertising works well in political campaigning because
    a. voters do not want to hear good things about candidates
    b. voters have selective attention for the candidates they support
    c. negative ads cost less to produce
    d. negative ads are more memorable than ones that praise the candidate's virtues

8. An interpretation of campaign events or election results that is most favorable to the candidate's position is called
    a. take
    b. analysis
    c. commentary
    d. spin

9. Studies have shown that
    a. the Internet will soon replace newspapers as the major source of agenda setting
    b. radio talk-shows are now setting the public agenda
    c. the media is losing its control over setting the public agenda
    d. the media plays an important part in setting the public agenda for government

10. Studies suggest that the early announcement of election results based on exit polls
    a. has had a great effect on the election outcomes
    b. has had a little effect on the election outcomes
    c. has had the most effect on presidential elections
    d. increases the interest of voters in the elections

11. The Telecommunications Act of 1996 was an attempt to regulate
    a. radio talk shows
    b. Hollywood movies
    c. indecent materials on the Internet
    d. violent professional sports on television

12. An unintended consequence of the Telecommunication Act of 1996 was
    a. more media choices for consumers
    b. V-chip controls included by TV manufacturers
    c. Digital TV mandates
    d. a race among competing corporate conglomerates to control media ownership

13. Thomas E. Patterson's analysis of bias in the media indicates that the real bias in the news is to
    a. recognize the liberal bias in news coverage
    b. emphasize bad news and cynicism
    c. recognize the conservative bias in news reporting
    d. emphasize in-depth reporting over generalized coverage

14. Kathleen Hall Jamieson's theory of media bias is based on a
    a. liberal bias
    b. conservative bias
    c. loser bias
    d. bad news bias

15. The "Daisy Girl" commercial form the 1964 presidential election campaign is a good example of
    a. spin
    b. managed news
    c. negative advertising
    d. narrow casting

16. The liberal bias in media is argued for by
    a. Professor Kathleen Jamieson
    b. Professor Thomas Patterson
    c. Pew Research Director Andrew Kohut
    d. CBS broadcaster Bernard Goldberg

17. Which of the "founding fathers" supported managed news?
    a. Thomas Jefferson
    b. Benjamin Franklin
    c. George Washington
    d. James Madison

18. Does the public have a right to media access?
    a. no, it is prohibited by the constitution
    b. no, it is prohibited by Congress
    c. Yes, it is specially stated in the 10th Amendment of the constitution
    d. Yes, the FCC and the courts support the concept

19. President George W. Bush establishment of military tribunals to prosecute suspected terrorists was
    a. ignored by the media
    b. strongly supported by the media
    c. criticized by the media, which led to change
    d. strongly supported by a government PR campaign, which overcame media objections

20. Alternate views of the news are more available today because of
    a. Talk Radio
    b. foreign newspapers
    c. underground newspapers
    d. the Internet

Short Essay Questions   Briefly address the major concepts raised by the following questions.

1. Describe the major functions performed by the mass media in our society.

2. Trace the historical development of media from the colonial period to modern times.

3. Describe the issues involved in the government's effort to regulate mass media.

4. Discuss the role of the media in political campaigns.

ANSWERS TO THE PRACTICE EXAM

Fill-in-the-blank

1.	entertaining the public	[p. 333]
2.	reporting the news	[p. 334]
3.	yellow journalism	[p. 338]
4.	narrow casting	[p. 340]
5.	television	[p. 341]
6.	sound bite	[p. 341]
7.	spin	[p. 343]
8.	press secretary	[p. 346]
9.	electronic, printed	[p. 347]
10.	citizens	[p. 348]

True/False

1.	F	[p. 335]	3.	T	[p. 340]	5.	T	[p. 344]	7.	F	[p. 347]	9.	F	[p. 347]
2.	T	[p. 336]	4.	F	[p. 341]	6.	T	[p. 345]	8.	F	[p. 347]	10.	T	[p. 349]

Multiple Choice.

1.	c	[p. 333]	6.	a	[p. 339]	11.	c	[p. 348]	16.	d	[p. 350]
2.	d	[p. 336]	7.	d	[p. 343]	12.	d	[p. 348]	17.	c	[p. 336]
3.	a	[p. 339]	8.	d	[p. 343]	13.	b	[p. 351]	18.	d	[p. 348]
4.	d	[p. 344]	9.	d	[p. 347]	14.	c	[p. 350]	19.	c	[p. 346]
5.	b	[p. 340]	10.	b	[p. 348]	15.	c	[p. 342]	20.	d	[p. 351]

Short Essay Questions   Briefly address the major concepts raised by the following questions.

1.   Describe the major functions performed by the mass media in our society. [p. 333-335].

- The mass media performs 6 basic functions. These are:
    - Entertainment, which has the most radio and television time, devoted to it.
    - Reporting the news, which is a primary function for all forms of media.
    - Identifying public problems, which means setting the public agenda for the government.
    - Socializing new generations, which is teaching young children and immigrants about American core values.
    - Providing a political forum for public information, and political campaigns. This is both for candidates and public officials, as well as for the public.
    - Making profits. The media in the United States is privately owned, but publicly regulated.

2.   Trace the historical development of media from the colonial period to modern times. [p. 335-341].

- The first medium was small politically sponsored newspapers that historians feel had an important role in unifying the country.
- The high-speed rotary press and telegraph produced mass produced newspapers, which were the first mass media. These papers often indulged in sensational biased journalism, known as yellow journalism.
- The electronic media began with the broadcast over radio of the 1920 presidential election returns.
- Television was first used in a significant way in the 1952 presidential election. Television has become the most influential and dominant medium.
- New trends in mass media, such as radio talk shows, cable and satellite television, and the Internet pose a real challenge to the dominance of network television.

3.   Discuss the role of the media in political campaigns. [p. 342-336].

- Media has made an obvious impact during political campaigns.
- One of the most effective political ads of all time was the "Daisy Girl" ad in the 1964 presidential campaign. This ad was the beginning of the negative ad campaign, which is so effective because views tend to remember these kinds of ads.
- The high cost of political ads has produced a need for a special media advisor to help candidates use or manage fee news coverage to their advantage. These advisors are called spin-doctors, and the way that they interpret the news in favor of their candidate is called spin.
- Presidential debates have been a staple of the political campaigns since the 1960 election. Image on television has become a key concern of all candidates.
- The media's impact on elections is hard to measure, but it seems to have the greatest impact on the undecided voter.

4.   Describe the issues involved in the government's effort to regulate mass media. [p. 347-348].

- The strong First Amendment protection of print media has not been provided to electronic media for a number of reasons.
- The Federal Communication Commission was created to regulate electronic media.
- The Telecommunication Act of 1996 ended the FCC rules that kept telephone companies from entering other kinds of communication businesses.
- The government has controlled the content of the broadcast media by encouraging the use of codes or standards of content. Provisions of the Telecommunication Act of 1996 provided for a "V-chip" to help parent's control the use of television by children, and attempted to regulate pornography on the Internet. The federal courts ruled that the provisions of the law applying to the Internet were unconstitutional.
- Both the FCC and the federal courts have ruled that the airwaves are public property, and that the public has a basic right to media access.

Chapter 12
THE CONGRESS

CHAPTER SUMMARY

Why was Congress Created?

The founders of the American Constitution believed that the bulk of government power should be in the hands of the legislative branch. The large and small state division at the constitutional convention created a bicameral Congress, with one house based on big-state population and the other based on small state equality in the senate. The differences between the institutions in this bicameral Congress were farther emphasized with a two-year term for Representatives in the House and a six-year term for Senators. [p. 359].

The Powers of Congress

The first seventeen clauses of Article I, Section 8 of the constitution specify most of the enumerated powers of Congress. Beyond these specific powers is the "necessary and proper" clause, which has allowed for a greatly expanded national government power. [p.360-361].

The Functions of Congress

Congress has six basic functions, which include, lawmaking, service to constituents, representation, oversight, public education, and conflict resolution. Lawmaking is the most obvious and important function of Congress. The idea for most legislation comes from outside, but Congress is solely responsible for approving legislation. Service to constituents is an important aspect of getting reelected, and is accomplished mostly by acting as an ombudsperson, and doing casework. A member can represent their constituency by being a trustee, who uses their own judgement, an instructed delegate, who uses the constituents judgement, or a politico, who uses both approaches depending on the issue. The oversight function is to make sure that the laws passed, are enforced and administered the way in which they were intended. The public education function is an important part of helping to set the public agenda, which primarily occurs with the media. See Chapter 11. The final function is to resolve conflicts in society, which primarily arise because of scarce resources, and differences in ideology. [P. 362-363].

House-Senate differences

Congress is composed of two very different but coequal chambers. The House is much larger at 435 members because it represents the population of the United States. The Senate is 100 members, which gives each of the fifty states, two senators. See Table 12-1 page 364, which shows the major differences between the House and the Senate. The size difference of the two, requires the House to have a Rules Committee to limit debate, while the Senate has unlimited debate, which sometimes leads to filibustering. The Senate, because of its smaller number and more powers from the Constitution, is considered the most prestigious to the institutions. [p. 363-365].

Congresspersons and the Citizenry: A Comparison

Members of Congress are more likely to be white, male, Protestant, and trained in higher-status occupations, than the average citizen is. [p. 365].

Congressional Elections

The process of electing members of Congress varies according to the election laws of each state, from which they are elected. Many congressional candidates are self recruited, and have ties to the local district. In recent years, the costs of campaigns have really escalated. Two major issues have a major impact of congressional elections. These are the presidential election years, which can produce a "coattails" effect, or a scandal, which can hurt the candidate, and the power of the incumbency, which makes it very difficult for a challenger to defeat the office holder. See Table 12-2, 366 on Midterm gains and losses, and Table 12-3, p. 367 on the power of Incumbency. The office holder can use advertising of their name recognition, claim credit for government programs, or take positions on popular issues. In spite of the advantage of incumbency, in the 1994 election, voters swept the Democratic majority in both chambers of Congress out of power. This development with Democrat Bill Clinton in the presidency, created a period of "divided government", which continued after the 2000 elections. [p. 365-368.]

Congressional Reapportionment

One of the most complicated aspects of congressional elections is the issue of reapportionment. Since representative in the House is based on population, after the census every ten years, the seat of the House must be allocated according to the latest population figures. This is called reapportionment. The state legislatures will redistrict or redraw political boundaries to match the changes that have occurred in population. In the past, legislatures did not always carry out this constitutional responsibility. In the **Baker v. Carr** case (1962), the Supreme Court ruled that this issue could be reviewed by the court, and that the legislatures had to use the principle of "one person, one vote" to redistrict. In **Reynolds v. Sims** (1964), the Court applied "one person, one vote" to both houses of the state legislature, and in **Wesberry v. Sanders** (1964), it was applied to Congress. One issue, which has not been fully resolved by the courts, is gerrymandering. This term refers to the manipulation of redistricting to give an advantage to one political party over the other one. [p. 369-373] See Figure 12-1, p. 370 and Figure 12-2, p. 372 for examples of different types of gerrymanders.

Pay, Perks, and Privileges

Members of Congress of congress receive a salary in 2002 of $150,000 a year, and receive a number of benefits, such as free parking, free medical care, generous pensions, liberal travel allowances, and free postage or franking privileges. They are able to hire an extensive professional staff, and use the resources of the professional staff of many other government agencies. Members of Congress are also exempt from certain laws that apply to the ordinary citizens. [p. 373-374].

The Committee Structure

The committees and sub-committees of Congress perform most of the actual work of creating legislation in Congress. Committees are commonly known as "little legislatures", because the committee is a microcosm of what happens in the legislature. There are five types of committees, standing, select, joint, conference, and the House Rules committee. Standing committees are the permanent committees, which are given a specific area of legislative policy. Select committees are created for a limited time period, and for a specific purpose. A joint committee is a composed of members of both the House and Senate. A conference committee is a special joint committee created to achieve agreement on legislation. See Table 12-4, p. 375 for a list of standing committees in the 108th Congress. The House Rules committee is unique to the House, and is necessary to set rules for the 435 members of the body. The leaders of House and Senate committees, called chairpersons, are selected by seniority among the members of the majority party in each chamber. [p. 374-376]

The Formal Leadership

The political parties organize the formal leadership of Congress. The leadership in the House is made up of the speaker, the majority and minority leaders, and party whips. The speaker of the House is the presiding officer of the House, a member of the majority party, and the most powerful member of the House. The majority leader is the leader of floor debate and cooperates with the speaker. The minority leader is the leader of the minority party, and speaks for the President, if the minor party controls the White House. Party officials called whips assist the leaders in Congress. The two most important formal leaders in the Senate are both ceremonial figures. The Constitution established the Vice-President as the presiding officer or President of the Senate. The Vice-President is rarely present for a meeting of the Senate. The Senate has elected a president pro tempore ("pro tem") to preside in the absence of the Vice-President. The real leadership power in the Senate is with the majority and minority floor leaders, which are assisted by whips. [p. 376-379]. See Table 12-5, page 379 for a complete list of the formal leadership structure in Congress

How Members of Congress Decide

It is difficult to establish all of the factors that determine how a member of Congress will vote. The single best predictor of how a member will vote seems to be political party membership. Party membership can be influenced by cues from respected senior members, regional and ideological differences. [p. 379-380].

How a Bill Becomes Law

The process of how a bill becomes law begins with the bill being introduced to the House or Senate or both. A bill is referred to the appropriate committee and subcommittee, where the heart of the legislative process occurs. The content specialists in the committee then closely examine a bill. If the bill is voted favorably by the committee, it will be sent to the Rules committee in the House or scheduled for floor debate in the Senate. The bill will be debated and voted on by the entire House and Senate. If a bill has passed the House and Senate with a majority vote in slightly different form, it will be sent to a conference committee to work out the differences in the bill. If approved by both the House and Senate, the bill will be sent to the president for his signature or veto. [p. 380]. See Figure 12-3, page 382 for an illustration of this entire process.

How Much Will the Government Spend?

The Constitution provides all that money bills must originate in the House of Representatives. Congress requires that the president prepares and submits the executive budget to Congress for their approval. Budget conflicts with the president, led Congress to pass the Budget and Impoundment Control Act in 1974. The federal government operates on a fiscal-year budget cycle that begins on October 1 each year. The Office of Management and Budget reviews each agency's budget request, and prepares a budget, which the president submit to Congress in January of each year. Congress then reviews the budget submitted by the president, and decides on the first budget resolution in May, which establishes the overall budget spending. The second budget resolution is supposed to be passed October 1, with the budget for each government agency. Often, Congress does not pass the second budget resolution by October 1. Congress must then pass a temporary law, called a continuing resolution, to keep government agencies open until the new budget can be agreed upon. [p. 380-385]. See Figure 12-4, page 383 for an overview of the budget process.

The Congress: Why Is It Important Today?

To many voters, Congress spends too much time in political battles. One of the most important decisions that Congress makes is how much the government spends. When members of Congress, go home to their districts, voters have the opportunity to argue for and against policy decisions. [p. 385]

KEY TERMS

Bicameralism – p. 359
Conference committee – p. 375
Constituent – p. 359
Enumerated power – p. 360
Filibustering – p. 364
Fiscal year (FY) – p. 383
Gerrymandering - p. 369

Instructed delegate – p. 362
Oversight – p. 362
Reapportionment – p. 369
Redistricting – p. 369
Seniority system – p. 376
Trustee - p. 362

OTHER RESOURCES

A number of valuable supplements are available to students using the Schmidt, Shelley, and Bardes text. The full list of the supplements is in the preface to this study guide. Ask your instructor how to obtain these resources. One supplement is highlighted here, the INFOTRAC Online Library.

INFOTRAC EXERCISES

Log on to http://www.infotrac-college.com.
Enter your Pass code that came with your textbook.
Use the CD that came with your textbook for suggestions for articles in this chapter.

PRACTICE EXAM
(Answers appear at the end of this chapter.)

Fill-in-the-Blank. Supply the missing word(s) or term to complete the sentence.

1. The Founding Fathers believed that the bulk of the power that the national government would exercise should be in the hands of the _____.

2. According to the thinking of the Founding Fathers, the House was to be the _____ _____ chamber and the Senate was to be the chamber of the _____.

3. The division of a legislature into two separate assemblies is _____.

4. The bulk of the bills that Congress acts upon originate in the _____ _____.

5. _____ is the process by which congress follows up on the laws it has enacted to ensure that they are being enforced and administered in the way Congress intended.

6. Under Senate Rule 22, debate may be ended by invoking _____ or shutting off discussion on a bill.

7. The impact that a strong presidential candidate has on the ballot is called _____.

8. _____ are by far the largest occupational group among congresspersons.

9. The process of electing members of Congress is controlled by _____
_____.

10. Committee chairs in congress are selected by _____.

True/False Circle the appropriate letter to indicate if the statement is true or false.

T F 1. The Founding Fathers believed that the bulk of the power of the national Government should be in the hands of the president.

T F 2. The principle function of any legislature is lawmaking.

T F 3. Instructed delegates mirror the views of the majority of the constituents whom elected them to power.

T F 4. The Rules Committee is the most powerful committee in the Senate.

T F 5. Members of Congress must be cautious about what they say on the floor of Congress, because of the possibility of being sued for slander.

T F 6. By far, the most important committees in Congress are the standing committees.

T F 7. Party membership is the single best predictor of how a member of Congress will vote on issues.

T F 8. If Congress does not approve a budget by the beginning of the fiscal year, the government can continue to operate on continuing resolutions.

T F 9. All money bills must originate in the House of Representatives.

T F 10. How much the government spends is the most serious issue for Congress today?

Multiple Choice   Circle the correct response.

1.   The Senate is the chamber of the Congress that
     a.   must first approve all money bills
     b.   must first approve amendments
     c.   ratifies treaties
     d.   has the first opportunity to override presidential vetoes

2.   The voting behavior of an instructed delegate would be to represent the
     a.   majority view of his or her constituents
     b.   broad interests of society
     c.   interests of his or her party
     d.   president in voting in Congress

3.   Some functions are restricted to only one house of Congress. The Senate is the only house that can
     a.   propose amendments
     b.   approve the budget
     c.   approve presidential appointments
     d.   investigate the president

4.   The <u>Central</u> difference between the House and the Senate is that the
     a.   House is much larger in membership than the Senate
     b.   House represents people, the Senate represents geography
     c.   Senate ratifies treaties
     d.   House first appropriates money

5.   The largest occupational group among congresspersons is
     a.   scientists
     b.   businesspersons
     c.   farmers
     d.   lawyers

6.   For the House of representatives,
     a.   each state is allowed two representatives
     b.   there is no set number of minimum or maximum for each state
     c.   each state is allowed at least one representative
     d.   membership for each state is determined by the House, itself.

7.   Most candidates for Congress must win the nomination for office in a
     a.   party caucus
     b.   indirect primary
     c.   direct primary
     d.   party convention

8.   Midterm Congressional elections
     a.   attract as many voters as presidential elections
     b.   attract more voters than presidential elections
     c.   usually result in the president's party losing seats in Congress
     d.   usually result in the president's party gaining seats in Congress

9. The Supreme Court cases of Baker v. Carr, Reynolds v. Sims, and Wesberry v. Sanders all pertained to the issue of
    a. foreign policy
    b. budget policy
    c. reapportionment
    d. campaign spending

10. The principle of "one person, one vote' was first applied to congressional districts in the Supreme Court case of
    a. Baker v. Carr
    b. Reynolds v. Sims
    c. Wesberry v. Sanders
    d. Plessy v. Ferguson

11. Gerrymandering refers to the process of
    a. ending debate in the Senate
    b. redrawing legislative boundaries
    c. forcing a bill out of committee
    d. selecting a committee chair

12. The phrase "little legislatures" refers to the
    a. legislatures that exist in the states
    b. committees in Congress
    c. departments of the federal bureaucracy
    d. interest groups that lobby Congress

13. The "third house of Congress" refers to
    a. standing committees
    b. select committees
    c. special committees
    d. conference committees

14. In the House of Representatives, the majority leader
    a. acts as spokesperson for the majority party in the House
    b. serves as Speaker of the House
    c. is elected in a vote of all the members of the House
    d. is rarely able to exert any meaningful leadership because of the dominance of the Speaker

15. The congressional budget process was very disjointed until the passage of the
    a. Office of Management and Budget
    b. Budget and Impoundment Control Act
    c. Discharge Petition
    d. Council of Economic Advisers

16. The fiscal year (FY) of the federal government is
    a. January to December
    b. April to February
    c. October to September
    d. July to June

17. The federal agency that prepares the budget is the
    a. Economic Agency
    b. Office of Management and Budget
    c. Congress
    d. Council of Economic Advisers

18. A continuing resolution allows
    a. congresspersons to remain in office after their term
    b. a nearly passed law to remain in the new session of Congress
    c. government agencies to continue to function, if a new budget is not passed
    d. the President to set the budget without Congress

19. The budget process of the federal government begins _____ before the start of the fiscal year.
    a. 1 to 1-1/2 years
    b. 2 years
    c. 6 months
    d. 3 months

20. One of the most important decisions for Congress, that affects our lives every day is
    a. under representation of minority groups
    b. how much the government spends
    c. reforming the Electoral College
    d. too many young people elected to Congress

Short Essay Questions   Briefly address the major concepts raised by the following questions.

1. Explain the major functions of Congress.

2. Trace the development of congressional reapportionment.

3. Describe the leadership positions in the House of Representatives and the Senate.

4. Discuss the steps that a bill must take to become law.

ANSWERS TO THE PRACTICE EXAM

Fill-in-the-blank

1.	legislature	[p. 359]
2.	common man's, elite	[p. 359]
3.	bicameralism	[p. 359]
4.	executive branch	[p. 361]
5.	oversight	[p. 362]
6.	cloture	[p. 364]
7.	"coattails"	[p. 366]
8.	lawyers	[p. 365]
9.	state legislatures	[p. 365]
10.	seniority	[p. 376]

True/False

1.	F	[p. 359]	3.	T	[p. 362]	5.	F	[p. 374]	7.	T	[p. 380]	9.	T	[p. 380]
2.	T	[p. 361]	4.	F	[p. 364]	6.	T	[p. 374]	8.	T	[p. 385]	10.	T	[p. 385]

Multiple Choice.

1.	c	[p. 360]	6.	c	[p. 365]	11.	b	[p. 369]	16.	c	[p. 383]
2.	a	[p. 362]	7.	c	[p. 366]	12.	b	[p. 374]	17.	b	[p. 383]
3.	c	[p. 360]	8.	c	[p. 366]	13.	d	[p. 375]	18.	c	[p. 385]
4.	a	[p. 363]	9.	c	[p. 369]	14.	a	[p. 378]	19.	a	[p. 383]
5.	d	[p. 365]	10.	c	[p. 369]	15.	b	[p. 383]	20.	b	[p. 385]

Short Essay Questions   Briefly address the major concepts raised by the following questions.

1. Explain the major functions of Congress. [p. 361-363].

- There are six major functions of Congress, which include lawmaking, service to constituents, representation, oversight, public education, and conflict resolution.
    - Lawmaking is the principal and most obvious function of a legislative body.
    - Service to constituents is primarily carried out by doing casework, and by acting as an ombudsperson with government agencies.
    - Members of Congress can represent constituents by being a trustee, or instructed delegate
    - The oversight function is for Congress to follow up on laws enacted, to see that they are being enforced and administered as intended.
    - The public education function of Congress is to assist in agenda setting.
    - Conflict resolution is a key function for government to resolve issues of scarce resources, and differences in societal goals.

2. Trace the development of congressional reapportionment. [p. 369-373].

- The process of reapportionment is the allocation of seats in the House of Representatives to each state after each census.
- The movement of people from rural areas to cities and suburbs created numerical malapportionment prior to 1960.
- In 1962, the Supreme Court in the case of **Baker v. Carr** ruled that the issue of reapportionment could be ruled on by the court on the basis of the "one person, one vote" principle.
- In 1964, the Supreme Court applied this principle to state legislatures in **Reynolds v. Sims**, and to congressional districts in **Wesberry v. Sanders**.
- Gerrymandering and "minority-majority" are issues of reapportionment that remain unresolved.

3. Describe the leadership positions in the House of Representatives and the Senate. [p. 376-379]. See Table 12-5, p. 379 for a complete list of the current individuals who hold leadership positions

    - Leadership in the House consists of the speaker, the majority and minority leaders and party whips.
        - The Speaker is the most important leader in the House, who presides, makes appointments, schedules legislation, decides points of order, and refers bills.
        - The majority and minority leaders are elected in party caucus and act as spokespersons, and leaders of their party.
        - Whips are assistants to the party leaders.
    - Leadership in the Senate consists of the vice-president, president pro tempore, majority and minority leaders, and party whips.
        - The Constitution creates the President of the Senate, the vice president, as the ceremonial leader of the Senate.
        - The Senate elects a ceremonial leader, president pro tempore, to preside over the Senate in the vice president's absence.
        - The real leadership power in the Senate rests with the majority and minority leaders.
        - Whips are assistants to Senate party leaders.

4. Discuss the steps that a bill must take to become law. [p 380]. See Figure 12-3, p. 382 for an illustration of the entire legislative process.

    - The bill is introduced to the House or Senate or both.
    - The bill is referred to the appropriate committee.
    - The bill is referred to subcommittee.
    - The full committee reports out the bill.
    - The Rules Committee in the House establishes rules for the bill.
    - The entire House debates the bill and vote on it.
    - The same steps, except for the Rules Committee, occur in the Senate.
    - Conference action may be required to clear up differences between the House and Senate.
    - The bill goes to the president for approval or veto.

Chapter 13
THE PRESIDENCY

CHAPTER SUMMARY

Who Can Become President?
The official requirements for becoming president are (1) a natural born citizen, (2) 35 years old, and (3) a fourteen year resident of the United States. The informal requirements suggest the president will be an older (54), white, Protestant male. [p. 393].

The Process of Becoming President
The voters do not directly vote for president and vice president, but instead vote for electors, who officially vote in the Electoral College. On a few occasions, the Electoral College has failed to elect a president, and the House of representatives have had to make the decision. The Twelfth Amendment adopted in 1804 clarified one aspect of this process by separating the election of the president and vice president. [p. 394].

The Many Roles of the President
The Constitution has created five major roles or functions for the president. These are (1) chief of state, (2) chief executive, (3) commander in chief of the armed forces, (4) chief diplomat, and (5) chief legislator. The chief of state role is the ceremonial head of state role. See page 395 for a list of these activities. The chief executive role requires the president to "faithfully execute" the laws.

The federal bureaucracy assists the president to carry out his executive responsibilities, and the president has appointive power to fill some government office positions. See Table 13-1, page 396 for a list of these positions. Under his executive power, the president can grant reprieves and pardons for all federal crimes, except in cases of impeachment. The president as commander in chief of the armed forces represents civilian control of the military. Presidents have probably exercised more authority in this role, than any other. In 1973, Congress attempted to gain more control over military actions with the War Powers Resolution. In spite of this resolution, the powers of the president as commander in chief are still extensive. The role of chief diplomat gives the president the power to recognize foreign government, to make treaties, with the approval of the Senate, and to generally conduct United States foreign policy. Presidents have greatly expanded their power in foreign policy through the use of executive agreements, which do not require Senate approval. The president's power as chief legislator consists of the annual state of the Union message, and the power of the veto. The vote power was expanded to include a line-item veto power on spending bills, which was first used by President Clinton. The law creating the line-item veto was challenged in the case of **Clinton v. City of New York**, and ruled unconstitutional in 1998 by the Supreme Court. See Table 13-2, p. 403 for a list of vetoes. Other presidential powers are given to the president by statute from Congress, express powers, and inherent powers defined through practice. [p.. 394-405].

The President as Party Chief and Superpolitician
Although the Constitution mentions nothing about political party leadership, the President is head of his political party. A major tool of the president as party leader is patronage. The president must be concerned about three different constituencies, as he leads his party. These constituencies are the public in general, the members of the political parties, and the Washington community. How successful the president is with these constituencies is measured by his approval rating. See Figure 13-1, p. 407 for a look at recent president's approval ratings. [p. 406-408]

The Special Uses of Presidential Power
Presidents have four special powers and privileges. These are (1) emergency powers, (2) executive orders, (3) executive privilege, and until recently, (4) impoundment of funds. The power to act in a crisis or emergency powers of the president were first stated in the Supreme Court case of **United States v. Curtiss-Wright Export Corp** in 1936. Executive orders issued by the president, which must be published in the Federal Register, have the force of law. Executive privilege is the right of executive officials to withhold information from legislative committees on the basis of separation of powers. This concept was upheld in 1974 by the Supreme Court case of **United States v. Nixon**. Nixon had to turn over the Watergate tapes,

because executive privilege could not be used to hide evidence in a criminal case. The concept did not hold up under President Clinton's impeachment proceedings. [p. 408-410]

The Abuses of Executive Power and Impeachment

The constitution authorized the House to impeach, and the Senate to remove the president, vice president, and other civil officials for "high Crimes and Misdemeanors". In the history of the United States, no president has been impeached and removed from office. President Andrew Johnson in 1868 was impeached, and tried by the Senate, which failed to remove him by one vote. In 1974, the House Judiciary Committee recommended impeachment charges against President Nixon over the cover-up of the Watergate break-in. Nixon resigned the presidency before the full House voted impeachment charges. In 1998, the House Judiciary Committee recommended an impeachment inquiry against President Clinton over the cover-up of the Monica Lewinsky affair. The articles of impeachment were then sent to the Senate, which conducted a trial and acquitted President Clinton. [p. 410-11].

The Executive Organization

At the beginning of Franklin Roosevelt's tenure as president, the staff was 37. Today, the staff is over 600. The advisory group for the president, called the cabinet, began with four officials. Today, there are 14 officials, including 13 secretaries of various departments, and the Attorney General. Modern presidents do not use the cabinet as an advisory group today, but prefer to rely on informal advisers, called the kitchen cabinet. In 1939, President Franklin Roosevelt created by executive order, the Executive Office of the President (EOP). The EOP consists of nine staff agencies that assist the president in carrying out all major duties. See p. 413 for a list of these agencies. One of the most important agencies in the EOP is the White House Office, which includes most of the key personnel and advisers to the president. In recent presidencies, the chief of staff is in charge of coordinating the White House Office. The Council of Economic Advisers (CEA) was created in 1946 to advise the president on economic matters. President Nixon created the Office of Management and Budget (OMB) from the Bureau of the Budget in 1970. This agency prepares the federal budget, and advises the president on management techniques. The National Security Council brings together the foreign policy and military advisers to the president. [p. 411-414]

The Vice Presidency

The Constitution only gives the vice president the duty to preside over the Senate and vote in case of a tie vote. Traditionally vice presidents have been selected to balance the ticket, and appeal to voters that the president does not appeal to. Eight times in our history, the vice-president has become president because of the death of the president. Each time this has happened, there was no provision to replace the vice president until the next election. Also there was no provision for a case of presidential incapacity. In 1967, the Twenty-fifth Amendment to the Constitution provided for both replacing the vice president, and a process for presidential incapacity. The first use of the amendment occurred with the resignation of Nixon's vice president, Spiro Agnew. Congress confirmed Gerald Ford as the new vice president. When President Nixon resigned the next year, Gerald Ford, became the first non-elected president in our history. President Ford selected with congressional approval, Nelson Rockefeller to be vice president. See Table 13-3, p. 417 for the line of succession to the Presidency. [p. 415-417].

The Presidency: Why Is It Important Today?

The scope of the presidency has changed from chief clerk to world leader in the twentieth century. The president has become a "super star" with the help of media, and the image often obscures important policy issues. The task of regulating the economy and overseeing the government has become very difficult with the advent of "divided government". The role of the president in engaging the nation in military action is another important issue that will remain in the new century. [p. 417].

KEY TERMS

Cabinet - [p. 412]
Chief diplomat - [p. 398]
Chief executive - [p. 395]
Chief legislator - [p. 401]
Chief of staff - [p. 394]
Commander in chief - [p. 397]
Council of Economic Advisers (CEA) - [p. 414]
Emergency power - [p. 408]
Executive agreement - [p. 401]

Executive Office of the President (EOP) - [p. 413]
Executive order - [p. 409]
Executive privilege - [p. 409]
Impeachment - [p. 411]
Line-item veto - [p. 404]
National Security Council (NSC) - [p. 414]
Office of Management and Budget OMB) - [p. 414]
Twenty-fifth Amendment - [p. 416]
White House Office - p. 414]

OTHER RESOURCES

A number of valuable supplements are available to students using the Schmidt, Shelley, and Bardes text. The full list of the supplements is in the preface to this study guide. Ask your instructor how to obtain these resources. One supplement is highlighted here, the INFOTRAC Online Library.

INFOTRAC EXERCISES

Log on to http://www.infotrac-college.com.
Enter your Pass code that came with your textbook.
You can access the article by typing the exact phrase below.

Executive Privilege
Clinton Misuse Executive Privilege
The premise of this article is President Clinton and members of his administration made repeated illegally use of executive privilege during the Lewinsky scandal in 1999.

Study Questions

1. What is executive privilege according to the Courts?
2. What specific examples of executive privilege did the article outline?
3. What is the author's conclusion about the Clinton use of executive privilege?

Impeachment
Do We Need a Twenty-Eighth Amendment?
The premise of this article is that the Twenty-Eighth Amendment is proposed by the author to clarify the existing constitutional procedures for Impeachment.

Study Questions
1. What were the problems with the Impeachment of President Clinton?
2. What changes in the constitution does the author propose?
3. Do you feel this amendment is needed?

PRACTICE EXAM
(Answers appear at the end of this chapter.)

Fill-in-the-Blank.   Supply the missing word(s) or term to complete the sentence.

1. The _____ Amendment clarified aspects of Electoral College voting.

2. The president decorating war heroes is an example of his role as chief _____ _____.

3. The president is constitutionally bound to enforce the acts of Congress, the judgements of federal courts, and treaties in his role as _____ _____.

4. The constitution gives the president the power to grant _____ and _____ for offenses against the United States except in cases of impeachment.

5. Presidential power in foreign affairs is greatly enhanced by the use of _____ _____ made between the president and other heads of state.

6. Powers given to the president by law are called _____ _____.

7. The formal indictment of the president for wrong doing by the House of Representatives is called _____.

8. The presidential advisory group composed of the secretaries of the executive departments is called the _____

9. The official responsible for coordinating the White House Office is the _____ _____ _____.

10. The only formal duty of the vice president found in the Constitution is to preside over the _____.

True/False   Circle the appropriate letter to indicate if the statement is true or false.

T   F   1. A presidential candidate can not win the Electoral College vote without getting a majority of the popular vote.

T   F   2. In most democratic governments, the role of chief of state is given to someone other than the chief executive.

T   F   3. The president's extensive appointment powers allow him to control and run the federal bureaucracy to suit his desires.

T   F   4. The president may grant reprieves and pardons for all offenses against the United States except in cases of contempt of Court.

T   F   5. The president has the sole power to recognize or refuse to recognize foreign governments.

T   F   6. Executive agreements made by the president and the heads of other governments must be ratified by the Senate.

T   F   7. The presidential veto is an effective legislative tool because Congress rarely can override them.

T   F   8. Emergency powers are the most common example of inherent powers exercised by the president.

T   F   9. An executive order is the president's legislative power.

T   F   10. Most presidents have relied heavily on their cabinet members for advice in decision making.

105

Multiple Choice   Circle the correct response.

1.   The most common occupation of presidents has been
      a.   teachers
      b.   lawyers
      c.   businessmen
      d.   farmers

2.   In the event that no candidate receives a majority of the Electoral College votes, the president is selected by the
      a.   Senate from the two candidates receiving the highest electoral votes.
      b.   Senate from any candidates receiving electoral votes
      c.   Congress from any person they choose to elect.
      d.   House of Representatives choosing from the highest three candidates receiving electoral votes

3.   The activity most typical of the Chief of State role is
      a.   developing military strategy
      b.   offering the State of the Union Address
      c.   negotiating treaties with foreign governments
      d.   receiving visiting chiefs of state at the White House

4.   The president can remove all of the following from office except
      a.   federal judges
      b.   the heads of cabinet departments
      c.   individuals within the Executive Office of the President
      d.   political appointees

5.   The effect of the Constitutional requirement that the president "shall be the Commander in Chief of the Army and Navy ," is to
      a.   require the president to be a commissioned officer
      b.   distort the lines of authority within the command structure of the armed forces
      c.   require the president to take instruction at one of the service academies
      d.   place the armed forces under civilian, rather than military, control

6.   The role in which the president has probably exercised more authority than in any other role is
      a.   Chief Administrator
      b.   Chief of his party
      c.   Commander-in-Chief
      d.   Chief Legislator

7.   The activity typical of the role of Chief Diplomat is
      a.   vetoing foreign policy legislation
      b.   delivering the State of the Union Address
      c.   meeting with state governors to discuss federal aid
      d.   negotiating treaties with foreign governments

8.   A typical activity associated with the role of Chief Legislator is
      a.   recognizing representatives from foreign governments
      b.   negotiating treaties with foreign governments
      c.   meeting with state party leaders to discuss campaign strategy
      d.   offering the annual State of the Union Address

9. The only requirement of a president in issuing an executive order is that the executive order must
    a. pertain to legislatively authorized items
    b. deal with only military matters
    c. deal only with the Executive Office of the President
    d. be published in the Federal Register

10. Executive privilege
    a. means that no member of the executive branch can be prosecuted for any act while they are performing their job
    b. is the concept that has been applied to the president's use of a pocket veto during a session of Congress
    c. protects the president and his cabinet from impeachment proceedings
    d. involves the ability of the president to withhold certain information from congress and/or the courts

11. The last president impeached by the House of Representatives was
    a. Lyndon Johnson
    b. Andrew Johnson
    c. Richard Nixon
    d. Bill Clinton

12. The agency that includes most of the key personal and political advisers to the president is in the
    a. Cabinet
    b. Congress
    c. White House Office
    d. National Security Council

13. Which statement is correct concerning the vice president's job?
    a. The Constitution gives several important powers to the vice president.
    b. The Constitution makes the vice president the number one advisor to the president.
    c. Earlier vice president had more to do than our recent vice president did.
    d. The constitution does not give much power to the vice president.

14. The Constitutional amendment establishing procedures for presidential succession and disability is the
    a. Twelfth Amendment
    b. Twenty-Fourth Amendment
    c. Twenty-Fifth Amendment
    d. Twenty-Seventh Amendment

15. The question of who shall be president if both the president and vice president die is answered by the
    a. Twenty-Fifth Amendment
    b. Special election to fill the vacancy
    c. Succession Act of 1947
    d. Twelfth Amendment

16. The only President to use the line-item veto was
    a. Reagan
    b. George H. Bush
    c. Clinton
    d. Nixon

17. The constituency that measures the presidential performance on a daily basis is the
    a. party constituency
    b. Congress
    c. Washington community
    d. media in rural areas

18. The style of presidential leadership has changed since World War II because of
    a. stronger political parties
    b. divided government
    c. the influence of television
    d. Post Modernity

19. The emergency powers of the president were confirmed in
    a. U.S. v. Curtiss-Wright Export Corp.
    b. Youngstown Steel and Tube Co. v. Sawyer
    c. U.S. v. Nixon
    d. Train v. City of New York

20. Which of the following is not in the Executive Office of the President (EOP)?
    a. White House Office Staff
    b. Office of the Vice President
    c. Council of Economic Advisers
    d. Office of Management and Budget

Short Essay Questions   Briefly address the major concepts raised by the following questions.

1. Identify and explain the roles of the president.

2. Trace the development of the sources of presidential power.

3. Describe the organization of the executive branch, and how it has evolved over time.

4. Discuss the evolving role for the vice president as an advisor and successor to the president.

ANSWERS TO THE PRACTICE EXAM

Fill-in-the-blank

1. Twelfth   [p. 394]
2. of, state   [p. 395]
3. chief executive   [p. 395]
4. reprieve, pardon   [p. 397]
5. executive, agreements   [p. 401]
6. statutory, power   [p. 404]
7. impeachment   [p. 411]
8. cabinet   [p. 412]
9. chief, of, staff   [p. 414]
10. senate   [p. 415]

True/False

1. F [p. 394]   3. F [p. 396]   5. T [p. 398]   7. T [p. 404]   9. T [p. 409]
2. T [p. 394]   4. F [p. 397]   6. F [p. 401]   8. T [p. 404]   10. F [p. 413]

Multiple Choice.

1. b [p. 393]   6. c [p. 398]   11. d [p. 411]   16. c [p. 404]
2. d [p. 394]   7. d [p. 400]   12. c [p. 414]   17. c [p. 406]
3. d [p. 395]   8. d [p. 401]   13. d [p. 415]   18. c [p. 408]
4. a [p. 396]   9. d [p. 409]   14. c [p. 416]   19. a [p. 408]
5. d [p. 397]   10. d [p. 409]   15. c [p. 417]   20. b [p. 413]

Short Essay Questions   Briefly address the major concepts raised by the following questions.

1. Identify and explain the roles of the president. [p. 394-404].

- There are five constitutional roles of the president. These are (1) chief of state, (2) chief executive, (3) commander in chief, (4) chief diplomat, and (5) chief legislator.
- The chief of state role consists of ceremonial functions, such as decorating war heroes, hosting chiefs of state, telephoning sports and space heroes, and dedicating parks.
- The chief executive role is to see that the laws are carried out. The president makes appointments of key individuals to carry out this function. He can also grant a reprieve and a pardon under executive authority.
- Commander in chief is the concept of civilian control of the military. This is probably the president's most powerful role.
- The chief diplomat role involves the making of treaties with the consent of the Senate, and recognizing foreign governments as legitimate.
- The chief legislator role includes the State of the Union message every year and the use of veto power in relationship to laws passed by Congress.

2. Trace the development of the sources of presidential power. [p. 404-405]

- There are four major sources of presidential power. These sources are (1) the Constitution, (2) statutes, (3) expressed power, and (4) inherent power.
- Constitutional powers of the president are contained in Article II, and are the powers discussed in essay one.
- Statutory power is created for the president through laws enacted by Congress, such the power to declare national emergencies.
- Expressed powers are those that are specifically written into the Constitution or laws.
- Inherent powers are those that can be inferred from loosely worded constitutional statements, such as "the executive power shall be vested in a President". Emergency powers invoked by the president during wartime are good examples of inherent powers.

3. Describe the organization of the executive branch, and how it has evolved over time. [p. 411-414].

- The administration of George Washington developed an advisory group, the cabinet, composed of the heads of the executive departments.
- Beginning with President Andrew Jackson, presidents used an informal group of advisors called the kitchen cabinet.
- President Franklin Roosevelt greatly expanded the administrative staff of the president by the creation of the Executive Office of the President (EOP) in 1939. The key parts of the EOP are
  - White House Office, which is coordinated by the chief of staff, and provides the president with what ever he needs to carry out his duties.
  - Council of Economic Advisers (CEA) advises the president on economic policy.
  - The Office of Management and Budget (OMB) prepares the budget and advises the president on management and planning.
  - The National Security Council advises the president on military and security issues.

4. Discuss the evolving role for the vice president as an advisor and successor to the president. [p. 415-417].

- The only role for the vice president mentioned in the Constitution is to preside over the Senate.
- Vice Presidents have traditionally been selected to balance the ticket.
- Eight vice presidents have become presidents because of the death of the president.
- The Constitution provided no process to select a new vice president.
- The Twenty-fifth Amendment provides for a process to select a new vice president, and for a case of presidential disability.
- The Succession Act of 1947 provides for the situation in which both the president and vice president die.

Chapter 14
THE BUREAUCRACY

CHAPTER SUMMARY

The Nature of Bureaucracy

Bureaucracy is defined as a large organization that is structured hierarchically to carry out specific functions. Bureaucracy can exist in both the public and private sectors. Public bureaucracies do not have a single set of leaders, are not organized to make a profit, and are supposed to maximize costs, and not necessarily be efficient and respond quickly to change. Bureaucracy in the United States enjoys a greater degree of autonomy than the bureaucracy in most other countries. The lack of government control of industry in the U.S. does not mean that administrative agencies do not regulate private industry. See Table 14-1, p. 423 for plans to end government inefficiency.

Models of Bureaucracy

There are several different theories about how bureaucracies function. The Weberian model viewed bureaucracies as rational, hierarchical organizations in which power flows from the top down. The Acquisitive model focused on the belief that top-level bureaucrats always try to expand their budget and staff. The Monopolistic model believed that bureaucracies are like monopolies in that they are less efficient and more costly to operate. The federal bureaucracy in the U.S. enjoys a greater degree of autonomy than in other countries because of its size, federal system, and lack of ownership of enterprises. [p. 424-425]

The Size of the Bureaucracy

The federal bureaucracy began with three departments, State, War, and Treasury, and the office of Attorney General in 1789, consisting of a handful of employees. Today, the fourteenth executive departments of government, and other agencies employ approximately 2.7 million employees. See Figure 14-1, p. 426 for a look at the government civilian employees by agency. [p. 425-426]

The Organization of the Federal Bureaucracy

The federal bureaucracy has four major types of structures. These are (1) cabinet departments, (2) independent executive agencies, (3) independent regulatory agencies, and (4) government corporations. The fourteen cabinet departments, described as line organizations, are the major part of the federal bureaucracy. See figure 14-3, p. 427 for the organization chart of the federal government. See Table 14-2, p. 429 for a list of executive departments. Independent executive agencies are bureaucratic organizations that are not part of an executive department, but still report directly to the president. See Table 14-3, p. 430 for the list, year created, and brief description of each agency. Independent regulatory agencies are responsible for regulating a particular sector of the economy in the public interest. The first agency established was the Interstate Commerce Commission (ICC) in 1887. See Table 14-4, p. 431 for the list, year created, and brief description of each agency. Government corporations are agencies that administer a quasi-business enterprise. The U.S. Postal Service is a good example of this type of bureaucratic structure. See Table 14-5, p. 432 for the list, year created, and brief description on each government corporation.

Staffing the Bureaucracy

There are two categories of bureaucrat, political appointees and civil servants. Political appointees are selected to the top positions in the government by the president. The average term of a political appointee is two years. The career civil servants, who make up the bulk of the bureaucracy can afford to wait out political appointees that they do not agree with. The federal civil service began in 1789 with a so-called natural aristocracy of society's "best citizens". When Andrew Jackson became President, he implemented the spoils system by awarding government jobs to his political supporters and friends. In 1883, the spoils system was reformed by replacing it with a merit system, and the Civil Service Reform Act or Pendleton Act was passed. This act created the Civil Service Commission to administer the personnel service. In 1939, the Hatch Act was passed to protect government workers from political manipulation. Finally, the Civil Service Reform Act of 1978 created the Office of Personnel Management (OPM), and the Merit Systems Protection Board (MSPB) . [p. 432-436]

Modern Attempts at Bureaucratic Reform

The government continues to attempt reforms of the bureaucracy, and make it more responsive to the needs of U.S. citizens. In 1976, congress passed the Government in the Sunshine Act. This law required all multiheaded federal agencies to conduct their business regularly in public session. Sunset legislation is designed to remove agencies on a regular basis, unless they are recreated with legislative action. This law has never been adopted by Congress, but most state legislatures have this law. Another approach to bureaucratic reform is contract out services from the private sector to produce more efficient service. The Government Performance and Results Act of 1997 was designed to improve efficiency in the federal work force. Agencies were to set goals, and establish a means of measuring if the goals were reached. The Merit Systems Protection Board (MSPB) created in 1978 was designed in part to protect whistleblowers, who would report bureaucratic waste and inappropriate behavior. [p. 436-440].

Bureaucrats as Politicians and Policymakers

Congress is unable to oversee the day-to-day administration of its programs. Congress delegates this authority to administrative agencies through what is called enabling legislation. Rulemaking by these agencies does not take place in vacuum, but occurs in the public arena because new regulations must be published in the Federal Register. Groups falling under regulation can engage in a process called negotiated ruling making. This process allowed individuals and groups to participate in the final rulemaking. Theories of bureaucracy once assumed that bureaucrats do not make policy decisions, but merely enforce these decisions. The concepts of iron triangle, and issue networks hold that bureaucrats do play a major role in policy decisions. [p. 440-444].

Congressional Control of the Bureaucracy

Although Congress cannot oversee the day-to-day operations of the bureaucracy, it can still control the bureaucracy by authorization and appropriation of funds, and by investigation and oversight hearings. [p. 444-445].

The Bureaucracy: Why Is It Important Today?

Attempts to reform bureaucracy will continue in the new century. Competition in the private marketplace will continue to influence government bureaucracy. The actual job of the federal bureaucracy will never disappear as long as government exists, and reforms will be needed on a continual basis to make the bureaucracy accountable to the citizens. [p. 445]

KEY TERMS

Acquisitive model - p. 424.
Bureaucracy - p. 423.
Civil Service Commission - p. 435.
Government corporation - p. 431.
Government in the Sunshine Act - p. 436
Hatch Act - p. 435.
Independent executive agency - p. 428.

Independent regulatory agency - p. 428.
Iron triangle - p. 444.
Issue network - p. 444.
Monopolistic model - p. 424.
Pendleton Act - p. 435.
Weberian model - p. 424.

OTHER RESOURCES

A number of valuable supplements are available to students using the Schmidt, Shelley, and Bardes text. The full list of the supplements is in the preface to this study guide. Ask your instructor how to obtain these resources. One supplement is highlighted here, the INFOTRAC Online Library.

INFOTRAC EXERCISES

Log on to http://www.infotrac-college.com.
Enter your Pass code that came with your textbook.
Use the CD that came with your textbook for suggestions for articles in this chapter.

PRACTICE EXAM
(Answers appear at the end of this chapter.)

Fill-in-the-Blank. Supply the missing word(s) or term to complete the sentence.

1. A _____ is the name given to a large organization which is structured hierarchically, and which is supposed to carry out specific functions.

2. The classic model of the modern bureaucracy is the _____ model.

3. The major service organizations of the federal government are the fourteen _____
    _____.

4. _____ _____ _____ are bureaucratic organizations that are not located within a department and report directly to the president.

5. The earliest independent regulatory agency to be created was the _____
    _____ _____.

6. The form of bureaucratic organization borrowed from business the _____
    _____.

7. The president generally associated with the spoils system is _____ _____.

8. Replacing government services with services from the private sector is called _____.

9. The three-way alliance among legislators, bureaucrats, and interest groups to benefit their respective interests is called the _____ _____.

10. The law that specifics the name, purpose, functions, and powers of an agency is _____
    _____.

True/False Circle the appropriate letter to indicate if the statement is true or false.

T   F   1. Modern presidents have been able to exert power over the bureaucracy in order to shape it to their own desires.

T   F   2. The federal bureaucracy in the United States is much more controlled and restricted than is true in other countries.

T   F   3. Cabinet departments can be described in management terms as line organizations.

T   F   4. Regulatory agencies are independent because they are administered independently of all three branches of government.

T   F   5. The assassination of President James Garfield had an impact on Civil Service Reform.

T   F   6. The Hatch Act prohibits federal civil service employees from engaging in political campaigns.

T   F   7. Today, few states have sunset laws.

T   F   8. Privatization of government services is a reform that has been most successful at the local level of government.

T   F   9. Today, agencies and departments of government do not play an important role in policymaking because of tight control by Congress.

T   F   10. Congress can call on the General Accounting Office to investigate bureaucratic agencies

Multiple Choice Circle the correct response.

1. A basic distinction between private corporations and public bureaucracies is that private corporations
   a. have managers and public bureaucracies do not
   b. are organized to make a profit and public bureaucracies are not.
   c. are efficient and public bureaucracies are not
   d. are generally large, complex enterprises, and Congress keeps public bureaucracies small.

2. The view that top-level bureaucrats will always try to expand the size of budgets is the theory of the
   a. Weberian Model
   b. Acquisitive Model
   c. Monopolistic Model
   d. Garage Can Model

3. The image of the bureaucracy as a noncompetitive organization is offered by the
   a. Garbage Can Model
   b. Acquisitive Model
   c. Monopolistic Model
   d. Weberian Model

4. Since 1970, most of the growth in government employment has occurred at the
   a. municipal level.
   b. State and local level
   c. National level
   d. County level.

5. The two groups of people in government who may call themselves bureaucrats are
   a. members of Congress and their appointees.
   b. The president and cabinet
   c. Political appointees and civil servants
   d. State employees and members of Congress

6. Thomas Jefferson brought into public service the so-called "natural aristocracy," which refers to
   a. a cadre of permanent civil servants
   b. permanent patronage appointments
   c. a small ruling clique whose membership is based on birth, wealth, and ability
   d. loyal servants

7. The Civil service Reform Act (Pendleton Act) had the effect of
   a. establishing in law the spoils system for political appointment
   b. establishing the principle of employment on the basis of open competitive exams
   c. preventing the best qualified people from being employed by the government
   d. allowing corruption and graft to enter the employment practices of government

8. The idea of sunset legislation was first suggested by President
    a. Franklin Roosevelt
    b. Jimmy Carter
    c. Abraham Lincoln
    d. Ronald Reagan

9. The major require imposed by the "Government in the Sunshine Act" is that
    a. federal agencies and commissions can have open meetings
    b. information and individuals and companies can be made public
    c. secret meetings may take place within the government
    d. all multi-headed federal agencies conduct their business regularly in public session

10. Sunset legislation refers to
    a. the idea that Congress must reauthorize programs annually
    b. legislation that protects a program so that the sun will never set on the program
    c. the idea of automatic program termination after a prescribed period unless Congress reauthorizes it
    d. built-in protections for program continuation

11. Congress created agencies within the federal bureaucracy to
    a. review proposed legislation
    b. implement legislation passed by Congress
    c. act as a sounding board for new laws
    d. control the actions of the president

12. The "iron triangle" refers to
    a. a policy of controlling information through censorship
    b. the alliance of mutual benefit formed between an agency, its client group, and congressional committees.
    c. the mathematical formula used by the bureaucracy to determine benefit payments
    d. an alliance between Congress, the president, and big business to control the economy

13. The ultimate check that Congress has over the bureaucracy is the ability to
    a. hire and fire members of boards and commissions
    b. write legislation in specific terms so that the bureaucracy will not be able to interpret the meaning of laws
    c. withhold the appropriations of money to the bureaucracy
    d. influence the president to take action against a bureaucrat

14. Negotiated rulemaking involves federal agencies in negotiations with
    a. Congress.
    b. the president.
    c. the courts.
    d. parties to be affected by a new rule.

15. Issue networks are
    a. another name for "iron triangles"
    b. a more complex concept than "iron triangles" that illustrates how experts support issues on a particular policy position.
    c. an attempt by the media to manipulate public opinion on a particular issue.
    d. insider relationships within Congress to protect congressional benefits.

16. An administrative unit directly accountable to the president is called a(n)
    a. Executive Office of the President (EOP)
    b. merit system
    c. line organization
    d. Bureau of the President (BOP)

17. The Hatch Act provided for
    a. testing workers to determine who should be hired
    b. prohibiting civil service workers from active political campaigning
    c. protection for whistleblowers
    d. privatization of government positions

18. Since Congress is unable to oversee the day-to-day administration of programs, it has
    a. created whistleblower legislation
    b. created enabling legislation
    c. created the Federal Register
    d. created "issue networks"

19. Negotiated rulemaking begins when an agency publishes the subject and scope of a new rule in the
    a. broadcast media
    b. "issue networks"
    c. Federal Register
    d. appropriate committee of Congress

20. Which of the following do not conduct investigation for Congress?
    a. congressional committees
    b. the Federal Register
    c. the General Accounting Office
    d. the Congressional Budget Office

Short Essay Questions   Briefly address the major concepts raised by the following questions.

1. Identify and explain several theories of bureaucracy.

2. Discuss the different types of government agencies and organizations in the federal bureaucracy.

3. Describe the recent reforms in the federal civil service.

4. Explain the iron triangle and issue network models of the bureaucracy.

ANSWERS TO THE PRACTICE EXAM

Fill-in-the-blank

1. bureaucracy   [p. 423]
2. Weberian   [p. 424]
3. cabinet departments   [p. 428]
4. Independent executive agencies   [p. 428]
5. Interstate Commerce Commission   [p. 428]
6. government corporation   [p. 431]
7. Andrew Jackson   [p. 434]
8. privatization   [p. 438]
9. iron triangle   [p. 444]
10. enabling legislation   [p. 440]

True/False

| 1. | F | [p. 428] | 3. | T | [p. 428] | 5. | T | [p. 434] | 7. | F | [p. 438] | 9. | F | [p. 442] |
| 2. | F | [p. 424] | 4. | T | [p. 430] | 6. | T | [p. 435] | 8. | T | [p. 438] | 10. | T | [p. 445] |

Multiple Choice.

1.	b	[p. 423]	6.	c	[p. 434]	11.	b	[p. 440]	16.	c	[p. 428]
2.	b	[p. 424]	7.	b	[p. 435]	12.	b	[p. 444]	17.	b	[p. 435]
3.	c	[p. 424]	8.	a	[p. 438]	13.	c	[p. 445]	18.	b	[p. 440]
4.	b	[p. 426]	9.	d	[p. 436]	14.	d	[p. 442]	19.	c	[p. 442]
5.	c	[p. 432]	10.	c	[p. 438]	15.	b	[p. 444]	20.	b	[p. 442]

Short Essay Questions

1. Identify and explain several theories of bureaucracy. [p. 424].

    *   There are three basic theories: (1) The Weberian model, (2) The Acquisitive model, and (3) The Monopolistic model.
        *   The classic or Weberian model viewed bureaucracy as rational, hierarchical organization in which power flows from the top downward and decisions are based on logic and data.
        *   The Acquisitive model focused on the concept that top level bureaucrats will want to maximize the size of their budgets and staff. The bureaucrat will try to "sell" their public service to Congress and the public.
        *   The Monopolistic model emphasized that bureaucracies are like monopolistic business firms, they have no competition. Monopolies tend to be less efficient and more costly to operate. This model arguing for the privatizing of some bureaucratic functions.

2. Discuss the different types of government agencies and organizations in the federal bureaucracy. [p. 428-432. See Tables 14-2, p. 429, 14-3, p. 430, 14-4, p. 431, and 14-5, p. 432.

    - There are four major types of bureaucratic structures. They are (1) cabinet departments, (2) independent executive agencies, (3) independent regulatory agencies, and (4) government corporations.
        - Cabinet departments are the fourteen executive departments, headed by a secretary, except for the Justice Department head by the Attorney General. These are the major service organizations of the national government.
        - Independent executive agencies are federal agencies not part of a cabinet department but report directly to the president. A good example of this kind of agency is the Central Intelligence Agency (CIA).
        - Independent regulatory agencies are agencies administered independently of all three branches of government, because they perform the functions of all three branches. A good example is the Federal Communication Commission (FCC), which regulates all communication by telegraph, cable, telephone, radio and television.
        - Government corporations are government agencies that administer a quasi-business enterprise. A good example is the U.S. Postal Service, which at one time was a cabinet department.

3. Describe the recent reforms in the federal civil service. [p. 436-440].

    - The important actual and proposed recent reforms include sunshine laws, sunset laws, contracting out, efficiency incentives, and more protection for whistleblowers.
        - Government in the Sunshine Act required all multi-headed federal agencies to hold public meetings.
        - Sunset laws require agencies to be terminated automatically at the end of a designated period, unless specifically reauthorized. This law has never been implemented by Congress, but most states have passed sunset laws.
        - Contracting out government services to private sector providers has been most successful at the local level for services like trash collection.
        - The Government Performance and Results Act of 1997 was designed to get government agencies to set goals, and create a measurement system to document if goals were reached.
        - In spite of the Whistle-Blower Protection Act of 1989, individuals, who bring to public attention gross government inefficiency or illegal action, are not protected from losing their job.

4. Explain the iron triangle and issue network models of the bureaucracy. [p. 444]

    - The iron triangle is a way of describing the bureaucracy's role in the policy making process.
        - It consists of a three-way alliance among legislators in Congress bureaucrats, and interest groups in a given policy area. Some examples are agricultural policy, weapon systems policy, and crime policy.
    - Issue networks is a more complex way to describe the bureaucracy's role in the policy making process.
        - An issue network consists of individuals or groups of experts that support a particular policy position on a given issue. This includes scholars, media, and others not usually considered part of the iron triangle theory.

Chapter 15
THE JUDICIARY

CHAPTER SUMMARY

The Common Law Tradition

The concept of common law originated in England as judge-made law, that is a body of law that grew out of judicial decisions shaped by prevailing custom. This concept has influenced the American judicial system. The two main components of common law are precedent, which is a court ruling that will bear on subsequent legal decisions in similar cases, and *stare decisis*, which means to stand on decided cases [p. 453].

Sources of American Law

The major sources of American law are federal and state constitutions, statutes passed by legislative bodies, administrative law, and case law. Constitutions set forth the general organization, powers, and limits of government. The U.S. Constitution is the supreme law of the land. Statutes or ordinances passed by national, state, and local governments have increasingly become important as courts apply these concepts to the general framework of common law. Case law is the rules and principles announced in court decisions, usually appeals courts [p. 454].

The Federal Court System

The United States has a dual court system, made up of the federal court structure and the courts of the fifty states. The federal courts are the U. S. district courts, which are the trial courts, thirteen U.S. courts of appeals, and the U.S. Supreme Court. See Figure 15-1, p. 456 for an overview of the federal court system. Figure 15-2, p. 457 shows the boundaries of the U. S. courts of appeals. The only court created in the U.S. Constitution is the Supreme Court, and it is the supreme law of the land. The state courts created by state constitutions are also under the authority of the U.S. Supreme Court. There is a common process that is followed by both court systems. The two parties in a lawsuit are the plaintiff, who initiates the suit, and the defendant, against whom the suit is brought. In recent years, interest groups have become more important in lawsuits, because they litigate, that is, bring the case to trial. Interest groups can also influence the judicial process by *amicus curiae* briefs, which express a group's viewpoint on the case. Class-action suits are also brought by groups to benefit all citizens who are affected by the same situation [p. 454-460].

The Supreme Court at Work

The Supreme Court term is from October to June each year. The Court is not required to hear a particular case, but several factors affect its decision. These factors include a legal question on which separate lower courts have ruled differently, and pressure from the solicitor general of the U.S. to review a case. The solicitor general represents the government in cases before the Supreme Court, and is sometimes referred to as the "Tenth Justice." The Court will issue a *writ of certiorari*, if it decides to hear a case. It takes four justices to agree to hear a case. This is called the rule of four. The Court decides a case by a process that begins with oral arguments by the attorneys representing the two parties. The justices will meet in private conference to discuss the arguments and decide the case. The decision can be unanimous, which happens rarely, or a majority decision, or a concurring opinion, in which a justice wishes to emphasize a particular part of the decision, or a dissenting opinion, which is important because it can form the basis for the creation of a new majority or precedent in the future. [p. 460-463.]

The Selection of Federal Judges

All federal judges are appointed by the president with the advice and consent of the Senate for a life time term. The concept of senatorial courtesy allows a senator of the president's political party to exercise control over the federal judge vacancies in his or her state, particularly for the district court positions. Senatorial courtesy does not apply to Court of Appeals and Supreme Court appointments. The Supreme Court appointments are among the most important appointments that the president makes. See Table 15-1, p. 465 for the background of Supreme Court justices. Ideology plays a major role in the selection process for federal judges. Most presidents select judges of their own political party and ideology for the federal courts.

Clinton has selected more women and members of minority groups to federal judgeships than any president before him. Ideology can also influence the Senate confirmation process. [463-466]

Policymaking and the Courts

The battles over judicial appointments reflect the growing importance of the judiciary in policymaking through the tool of judicial review. Judicial review was established by the Supreme Court's decision in *Marbury v. Madison* (1803). Judges hold different views of the Court's role in policymaking. Judicial activism is a doctrine holding that the Supreme Court should take an active role in using its powers to check the other institutions of government when they exceed their authority. Judicial restraint rests on the principle that the Court should defer to the decisions made by the institutions elected by the people. The current court named for Chief Justice William Rehnquist, is a more conservative court than in the past. President Clinton's appointments to the court have brought about a more balanced court between liberal and conservative. See textbook for the current court members and ideological breakdown on page 470. The extensive influence of the Court today has produced a public debate about the amount of power the court has. Some critics want to see the power of the Court reduced [p. 467-472].

What Checks Our Courts?

The executive, the legislature, the public, and the judiciary itself check the power of the courts. The executive branch carries out judicial rulings; the court does not have enforcement powers. The president also exercises control over the federal courts by his appointment of new judges. Congress must authorize funding to implement court decisions, and can pass new laws in response to court decisions, or begin the constitutional amendment process. Public opinion can limit the power of the court, since it has no enforcement powers; its authority is linked to its stature in the eyes of the public. Finally, the traditions of the court, including its refusal to hear political questions, which the court believe should be decided by the elected branches. All these factors offer protection to the public from excessive court power [p. 472-475].

The Judiciary: Why Is It Important Today?

The judiciary through judicial provides a check on the power of Congress and the president. The Court has interpreted the constitution to provide for concepts such as the right to privacy. The judiciary is also important for providing stability to our society by allowing controversial issues to be decided in a peaceful way. [p. 475]

KEY TERMS

amicus curiae brief—p. 459
appellate court—p. 457
class-action suit—p. 459
common law—p. 453
concurring opinion—p. 463
dissenting opinion—p. 463
judicial activism—p. 467
judicial restraint—p. 468

majority opinion—p. 463
oral arguments—p. 462
precedent—p. 453
rule of four—p. 462
senatorial courtesy—p. 463
stare decisis—p. 453
unanimous opinion—p. 463
writ of certiorari—p. 462

OTHER RESOURCES

A number of valuable supplements are available to students using the Schmidt, Shelley, and Bardes text. The full list of the supplements is in the preface to this study guide. Ask your instructor how to obtain these resources. One supplement is highlighted here, the INFOTRAC Online Library.

INFOTRAC EXERCISES

Log on to http://www.infotrac-college.com.
Enter your Pass code that came with your textbook.
Use the CD that came with your textbook for suggestions for articles in this chapter.

PRACTICE EXAM
(Answers appear at the end of this chapter.)

Fill-in-the-Blank. Supply the missing word(s) or term(s) to complete the sentence.

1. The body of judge-made law that developed from England and is still used today in the United States is called _____ _____.

2. The practice of deciding new cases with reference to former decisions is based upon the doctrine of _____ _____.

3. The United States' dual court system consists of both _____ courts and _____ courts.

4. The Supreme Court's decision to hear a case is determined by the rule _____ _____.

5. A _____ _____ suit filed by an individual seeks damages for "all persons similarly situated."

6. By _____ of _____ the Supreme Court orders a lower court to send it the record of a case for review.

7. A _____ opinion is an opinion written by a Supreme Court justice who agrees with the majority opinion but for different reasons.

8. About 20% of Supreme Court appointments are _____ by the Senate.

9. Court decisions are translated into action by _____ _____.

10. Justices advocating the doctrine of _____ _____ believe the Supreme Court should defer to decisions made by elected representatives.

True/False. Circle the appropriate letter to indicate if the statement is true or false.

T   F   1. Most of American law is based on the English legal system.

T   F   2. Case law includes judicial interpretations of common law.

T   F   3. Federal court jurisdiction is less limited than state court jurisdiction because the federal government has jurisdiction over all the country.

T   F   4. Federal courts have authority to rule on all issues relating to state laws and federal matters.

T   F   5. Interest groups no longer use *amicus curiae* briefs to influence Supreme Court decisions.

T   F   6. Federal judges are either appointed or elected depending upon the type of court.

T   F   7. The nomination of Supreme Court justices belongs solely to the president.

T   F   8. Ideology no longer plays a very important role in a president's choice for the Supreme Court.

T   F   9. The makeup of the federal judiciary is typical of the American public.

T   F   10. The ideology of the Rehnquist court is more conservative with respect to states' rights.

Multiple-Choice. Circle the correct response.

1. *Stare decisis* is a doctrine
   a. enabling court decisions to vary from case to case.
   b. providing guidance to judges when common law does not apply.
   c. encouraging the following of precedent or previous court decisions.
   d. requiring hearings about complaints arising from regulations.

2. The level of trial courts in the federal judicial hierarchy is the
   a. District courts.
   b. Court of Appeals.
   c. Supreme court.
   d. state courts.

3. Appellate jurisdiction means the authority of a court to
   a. serve as a trial court.
   b. hear cases for the first time.
   c. review decisions from a lower court.
   d. establish grand juries.

4. A *writ of certiorari* is defined as an order
   a. compelling an official to carry out his responsibilities.
   b. guaranteeing the right to a fair and impartial trial by jury.
   c. preventing some action from being carried out.
   d. to a lower court to send a case to the higher court for review.

5. A *writ of certiorari* is issued by the Supreme Court only when
   a. a majority of justices vote for such a request.
   b. four justices vote for such a request.
   c. a unanimous Court supports such a request.
   d. the Solicitor General approves such a request.

6. The official who represents the national government in the Supreme Court is the
   a. Attorney General.
   b. Solicitor General.
   c. Vice-President.
   d. Chief Justice.

7. A Justice who accepts the majority decision, but not the reasons for it, may write his/her own
    a. minority opinion.
    b. majority opinion.
    c. *amicus curiae* opinion.
    d. concurring opinion.

8. In terms of enforcement powers, the Supreme Court
    a. has now acquired its own police force.
    b. relies upon the good will of the public to see that its decisions are enforced.
    c. must rely on other units of government to carry out its decisions.
    d. does not make decisions that have to be enforced.

9. Dissenting opinions in a Supreme Court decision are important because
    a. they allow justices to make symbolic statements.
    b. they agree with the majority opinion, but for different reasons.
    c. they often form the basis for arguments that reverse decisions and establish new precedent.
    d. they allow opposition groups to express their opinions before the court.

10. Senatorial courtesy is a concept that
    a. allows the president to pick his choice for judge
    b. can veto a presidents choice for judge
    c. applies only to Supreme Court nominations
    d. applies only to state court nominations

11. The courts that have become "stepping-stones" to appointment to the Supreme Court are the
    a. District Courts.
    b. State Supreme Courts.
    c. Courts of Appeals.
    d. Tax Court.

12. In terms of judicial philosophy, Chief Justice William Rehnquist is know as a
    a. liberal justice.
    b. swing vote.
    c. conservative justice.
    d. moderate pragmatist.

13. The justices who believe that the Court should use its power to alter or challenge the policy direction of Congress, state legislatures, or administrative agencies are advocating
    a. judicial restraint.
    b. judicial activism.
    c. strict constructionism.
    d. moderate pragmatism.

14. The tradition of the Court has led justices to refuse to hear cases which are
    a. justiciable disputes.
    b. political questions.
    c. between citizens of different states.
    d. a real controversy.

15. The appointments of President Clinton to the Supreme Court have elevated the number of
    a. women to record numbers.
    b. Democrats to record numbers.
    c. minority members to record numbers.
    d. liberal members to record numbers.

16. Case law refers to
    a. a case involving federal law
    b. a case heard by the Supreme Court
    c. rules and principles announced in court decisions
    d. a justiciable dispute

17. The concept of judicial review was established in the case of
    a. Marbury v. Madison
    b. McCulloch v. Maryland
    c. Common law
    d. Brown v. Board of Education of Topeka

18. In several 2000 cases, the Supreme Court ruled that _____ had overreached authority under the commerce clause.
    a. the President
    b. Congress
    c. State governments
    d. Federal bureaucracy

19. A justiciable dispute or controversy is
    a. the same as a political questions
    b. the same as *stare decisis*
    c. disputes that arise out of actual cases
    d. a case decided by the Supreme Court

20. The U.S. Supreme Court overturning the Florida Supreme Court over vote counting in the 2000 Presidential election, surprised many observers because
    a. of judicial review
    b. of support of Civil Rights cases
    c. of support of rights of Accused cases
    d. of support of state rights cases

Short Essay Questions. Briefly address the major concepts raised by the following questions.

1. Identify and explain the common law tradition and other major sources of American law.

2. Discuss the process the Supreme Court uses to decide cases.

3. Describe the presidential appointment process for federal judges.

4. Explain the checks or limitations on the power of the federal courts.

ANSWERS TO THE PRACTICE EXAM

Fill-in-the-Blank

1. common law   [p. 453]
2. *stare decisis*   [p. 453]
3. state, federal   [p. 454]
4. of four   [p. 462]
5. class-action   [p. 459]
6. *writ of certiorari*   [p. 462]
7. concurring   [p. 463]
8. rejected   [p. 466]
9. judicial implementation   [p. 472]
10. judicial restraint   [p. 468]

True/False

1.	T	[p. 453]	3.	T	[p. 456]	5.	F	[p. 459]	7.	T	[p. 464]	9.	F	[p. 465]
2.	T	[p. 454]	4.	F	[p. 456]	6.	F	[p. 463]	8.	F	[p. 466]	10.	T	[p. 471]

Multiple Choice

1.	c	[p. 453]	6.	b	[p. 462]	11.	c	[p. 464]	16.	c	[p. 454]
2.	a	[p. 457]	7.	d	[p. 463]	12.	c	[p. 470]	17.	a	[p. 467]
3.	c	[p. 457]	8.	c	[p. 472]	13.	b	[p. 467]	18.	b	[p. 471]
4.	d	[p. 462]	9.	c	[p. 463]	14.	b	[p. 475]	19.	c	[p. 475]
5.	b	[p. 462]	10.	b	[p. 464]	15.	a	[p. 466]	20.	d	[p. 471]

Short Essay Answers. An adequate short answer consists of several paragraphs that discuss the concepts addressed by the question. Always demonstrate your knowledge of the ideas by giving examples. The following represent the major ideas that should be included in these short essays.

1. Identify and explain the common law tradition and other major sources of American law [p. 453-454].

    *   Common law is a body of judge-made law that originated in England from decisions shaped according to prevailing custom.
    *   The other major sources of American law are federal and state constitutions, statutes, administrative law, and case law.
    *   Constitutions set forth the general organization, powers, and limits of government.
    *   Statutes are laws enacted by any legislative body at federal, state, or local level.
    *   Rules and regulation issued by administration agencies are a source of law.
    *   Case law includes judicial interpretations of all of the above sources of law.

2. Discuss the process the Supreme Court uses to decide cases [p. 460-463].

   - The Supreme Court term begins in October and adjourns usually in June.
   - The first important decision for the Court is to decide which cases to hear.
   - Important factors to consider are whether a legal issue has been decided differently by two separate courts, and if the Solicitor General is pushing the case.
   - If the Court decides to hear a case, four justices (Rule of four) must agree to issue a *writ of certiorari*.
   - Oral arguments will be scheduled before the Court when attorneys representing each side will present their cases.
   - A private conference will be held in which the justices discuss the case and decide on an opinion.
   - Opinions can be unanimous, majority, concurring, and dissenting.

3. Describe the presidential appointment process for federal judges [p. 463-466].

   - All federal judges are appointed by the president for life terms, with Senate advice and consent.
   - The first step in the process is nomination by the president.
   - Senatorial courtesy can be a big factor in the nomination of federal district judges. A senator of the president's party has a great deal of influence over federal district judge appointments from the senator's state. Senators have less influence over appeals court nominees, and no influence on Supreme Court appointment.
   - Ideology and political party background are two of the most important factors determining who is nominated for federal judgeships.

4. Explain the checks or limitations on the power of the federal courts [p. 472-475].

   - Our judicial system is probably the most independent in the world, but there are important checks on the power of the courts. These checks are the executive, the legislature, the public, and the judiciary itself.
   - The executive branch has the power of judicial implementation. The way in which court decisions are translated into action is solely the responsibility of the executive branch.
   - Court rulings can be modified or overturned by lack of appropriations to carry out rulings, or
   - Overturned by constitutional amendments.
   - Public opinion is an important factor, since the Court has no enforcement powers; its authority is linked to its stature in the eyes of the public.
   - Federal judges typically exercise self-restraint in making their decisions. Political questions are issues that a court defers to the decision-making of the executive or legislative branches.

Chapter 16
DOMESTIC AND ECONOMIC POLICY

CHAPTER SUMMARY

The Policymaking Process

The beginning of the policymaking process is the recognition that a problem exists and needs a solution. The Aviation Security Act of 2001 provides a good example of the creation of a policy. There are five basic steps in policymaking:

- agenda building
  The crisis of 9/11 put the issue on the agenda immediately after the attacks.
- agenda formulation
  Members of Congress worked closely with representatives from a number of groups and trade associations, such as the airline industries, pilots, private security contractors, and others.
- agenda adoption
  Congress passed the Aviation Security Act federalizing airport security in 2001.
- agenda implementation
  The major provisions of the law called for airport screening workers to apply to the federal government for employment. New screening equipment will take months or years to finally be installed.
- agenda evaluation [p. 465].
  Evaluation continues, and Congress will receive feedback on the results of the Act. [p. 485-487]

Poverty and Welfare

Historically, poverty has been accepted as inevitable. Industrialized wealthy nations like the United States have been able to eliminate mass poverty through income transfers. An array of welfare programs transfer income from wealthy to poor individuals. The official definition of poverty in the United States is $16,500 yearly income for an urban family of four. The poverty level varies with family size and location. See Figure 16-1, p. 4, for a look at the official poverty numbers since 1959. In-kind subsidies, such as food stamps, low-income housing, and medical care are not usually counted as income. If these benefits are counted as income, the poverty rate drops. In the wake of the Welfare Reform Act of 1996, the U.S. government provides the following low-income assistance: Temporary Assistance to Needy Families (TANF), Supplemental Security Income (SSI), food stamps, and the earned-income tax credit (EITC) program The Welfare Reform Act of 1996 gave states more control over welfare programs, but at the same time created major new problems for states to solve. The provisions of the law conflict with many state constitution mandates to take care of the needy, and require more enforcement provisions that states must pay for. The long-term effects of a loss of income to children in poor families may cause severe problems in the future. Finally, the loss of income may add to the problem of homelessness in the United States [p. 487-491]].

Crime in the Twenty-first Century

Crime has been a major policy concern since the time of the American Revolution. Two crime issues that have been particularly significant are the rise in violent crimes and the increasing number of serious crimes committed by juveniles. One of the major costs of fighting crime is building new jails and prisons. Illegal drugs are recognized as a major source of crime. Two frequently mentioned methods of solving the drug problem are the get-tough policy of involving major new resources, such as the military, and the legalizing of drugs to take away the economic incentive. A third alternative is to allow states to experiment with these two different approaches. Terrorism has jumped to the top of crime concerns with the attacks on the World Trade Center and the Pentagon on September 11, 2001. Laws have been passed such as the Aviation Security Act, but it is too early to tell if these will be effective on the war on terrorism [p. 491-495].

Environmental Policy

The impact of human action on the environment has been a concern in the twentieth century with industrialization and population increases. Federal legislation began in the 1960s to protect the environment. See Table 16-1, p. 496 for a list of major federal environmental legislation. The first major environmental legislation, caused by the Santa Barbara oil spill in 1969, was the National Environmental

Policy Act. This act provided for an environmental impact statement (EIS) of major federal actions that might affect the quality of the environment   The Clean Air Act of 1990 addressed the air pollution caused by acid rain. The economic costs have become a significant political issue in the past two decades. [495-498]

The Politics of Economic Decision Making

Public policymaking is complicated, and nowhere is that more apparent than in economic policy where each policy action carries costs and benefits, known as policy trade-offs. In the world of taxes and subsidies, for every action on the part of government there is a reaction on the part of the affected public. This is known as the action-reaction syndrome. Individuals and corporations facing high taxes will have a big incentive to find or add loopholes to the tax laws. See Table 16-2, p. 498 for 2002 tax rates. The 2001 legislation to lower the tax rates was undermined by adding new loopholes to the tax laws.

The question of taxes in America always raises a discussion of the Social Security tax. The tax on employees and employers is a regressive tax in which people with higher incomes pay lower tax rates than people with lower incomes. The program is basically a pay-as-you-go transfer system in which those who are working pay benefits to those who are retired. The number of people working is declining relative to the number of people retiring, and the large numbers of the baby boom generation will bankrupt the current system when they retire beginning in the early twenty-first century. See figure 16-2, and 16-3, p. 501 on Medicare costs, and workers per retiree. Numerous proposals to save the Social Security system have focused on allowing individuals to make private investments of social security taxes. See figure 16-4, p. 502 on private rates of return. No policy decision has been made, but a decision must be made, as nothing can be done to stop the aging of the population [p. 500-503].

Changes in taxes are sometimes part of an overall fiscal policy change. A fiscal policy is the use of government spending or taxation to alter the national economy. One approach to fiscal policy is to use government funds to stimulate economic activity in a recession by increasing expenditures and decreasing taxes. Known as Keynesian economics, this policy grew out of the theories of the English economist John Maynard Keynes. Conversely, during inflation, the government should reduce spending and increase taxes to balance the economy.

A monetary policy is also used to alter the economy by controlling the amount of money in circulation, which can affect interest rates, credit, inflation, and employment. Monetary policy works in a similar way to fiscal policy. In times of recession, the economy is stimulated by a greater supply of money and credit. With inflation, the money supply, and hence credit, is reduced to bring down the level of economic activity. The Federal Reserve System, called the Fed and created in 1913, largely carries out monetary policy. The chairperson of the system usually speaks for the entire board. The Fed and its Federal Open Market Committee (FOMC) make decisions about monetary policy eight times a year. Although monetary policy can be implemented much quicker than fiscal policy, it still seems to take over a year to affect the economy. In recent years, the Fed's record has been mixed at best, as some actions seem to have affected the economy in the wrong way [p. 503-505].

Budget Deficits and the Public Debt

Until the late 1990s, the federal government had run a deficit in every year except two since 1960. A deficit results from spending more than revenues allow, and issuing U.S. treasury bonds to borrow the difference. The accumulation of all past deficits is known as the national debt or public debt and has been a major policy issue. See Table 16.3, p. 505 for net public debt totals. While the government cannot go bankrupt as long as it makes interest payments, public debt financing by selling bonds can "crowd out" private borrowing and slow the rate of economic growth. See Figure 16-5, p. 505 for a look at public debt as a percentage of national output. In 2001, the economy was beginning a recession, when terrorists attacked the Pentagon and the World Trade Center towers. Government expenditures increased dramatically, and federal government deficits have returned for many years to come. [p. 505-506]

America and the Global Economy

At the close of World War II, the United States was the most powerful economy in the world. This situation continued for twenty-five years. In the last few decades, Japan, the European Union, and other nations of the Pacific Rim have challenged U.S. dominance in the global marketplace. The current situation seems to be favorable to the United States even with a big deficit in balance of trade. In the late 1990s, many of the Asia, and European economies were stagnating. Clearly, the United States remains among the premier world economy powers, but can no longer take this position for granted. [506-508]

Domestic and Economic Policy: Why Is It Important Today?
The issues of welfare reform and immigration have been linked in policy debate, as many legal and illegal immigrants receive benefits. Social Security will continue to be a major issue as our population continues to age. Crime and balancing economic growth with the protection of the environment will continue to be important issues well into the next century [p. 508].

KEY TERMS

action-reaction syndrome—p. 498
domestic policy—p. 485
earned-income tax credit (EITC)—p. 490
environmental impact statement (EIS)—p. 496
Fiscal policy---p. 503
food stamps—p. 489
income transfer—p. 487

in-kind subsidy—p. 488
monetary policy---p. 503
policy trade-offs---p. 498
public debt---p. 505
Supplemental Security Income (SSI)—p. 489
Temporary Assistance to Needy Families
(TANF)—p. 489

OTHER RESOURCES

A number of valuable supplements are available to students using the Schmidt, Shelley, and Bardes text. The full list of the supplements is in the preface to this study guide. Ask your instructor how to obtain these resources. One supplement is highlighted here, the INFOTRAC Online Library.

INFOTRAC EXERCISES

Log on to http://www.infotrac-college.com.
Enter your Pass code that came with your textbook.

Bush Bilks Elderly p. 329
The premise of this article is that President Bush spending proposals will provide a tax cut for the Wealthy and seriously damage Social Security, and Medicare.

Study Questions
1. What is President Bush plan for Medicare?
2. What is the current situation with Social Security?

Faith-Based Action p. 335
The premise of this article is that President Bush proposal to provide government funds for faith-based organizations to solve social problems will impact different political groups.

Study Questions
1. What is the trend toward faith-based action for social problems?
2. What political groups does the author analyze?
3. What are obstacles that these groups bring to the successfully implementation of this policy?

Let Bullies Beware p. 336
The premise of this article is that schools across the country have developed programs to deal with the problem of school bullies.

Study Questions
1. How does changing the school culture impact bullies?
2. Why are school bullies such an educational problem?
3. Review the poll at the end of the article. Which group would you put yourself in?

PRACTICE EXAM
(Answers appear at the end of this chapter.)

Fill-in-the-Blank. Supply the missing word(s) or term(s) to complete the sentence.
1. Courses of action on issues of national importance are called _____ _____.

2. Selecting a specific strategy in the policymaking process is referred to as _____ _____.

3. The attacks of 9/11 resulted in the _____ _____ Act of 2001.

4. A traditional solution to poverty has been _____ _____.

5. The issue of crime has been on the national agenda in the U. S. for _____ .

6. A disturbing element of crime in the U.S. is the number of serious crimes committed by _____.

7. The majority of arrests today in the U.S. are for crimes related to _____ _____.

8. The U.S. government has been addressing pollution since before the _____ _____.

9. The major environmental law prompted by the Santa Barbara oil spill was the _____ _____ _____ _____.

10. Individuals and corporations facing high taxes will always react by making concerted efforts to get Congress to insert _____ in new tax laws.

True/False. Circle the appropriate letter to indicate if the statement is true or false.

T   F   1. The first step in the policymaking process is getting the issue on the agenda.

T   F   2. Historically throughout the world, poverty has been accepted as inevitable.

T   F   3. The poverty rate today is based on the consumer price index (CPI).

T   F   4. Food stamps are given only to the elderly and disabled.

T   F   5. The problem of homelessness has almost disappeared in the 21st century.

T   F   6. Polls indicate that most Americans are worried about violent crime.

T   F   7. Ozone is the basic ingredient of smog.

T   F   8. Only recently has the U.S. government begun to respond to the problems of pollution.

T   F   9. The United States is making fairly substantial strides in the war on toxic emissions.

T   F   10. One consequence of federal debt financing is that it tends to crowd out private borrowing.

Multiple-Choice. Circle the correct response.

1. The first step in solving a public problem is
   a. to determine the cost involved.
   b. to determine who will be helped and who will be harmed.
   c. for people to become aware of the problem.
   d. for the President to declare a state of emergency.

2. After public policy implementation, the last step is
   a. the variables associated with cost analysis.
   b. Policy evaluation
   c. the ease with which solutions can be accomplished.
   d. Policy formulation

3. A traditional solution to eliminate poverty has been
   a. work programs.
   b. payment vouchers.
   c. education training programs.
   d. Income transfer.

4. The United States has been able to eliminate mass poverty because of
   a. foreign aid from other countries.
   b. sustained economic growth.
   c. in increased work ethic.
   d. mass infusions of tax dollars.

5. The threshold income level for defining poverty was originally based on
   a. the consumer price index.
   b. the cost of a nutritionally adequate food plan by the U.S. Dept. of Agriculture.
   c. guidelines established by the Consumer Protection Agency.
   d. guidelines from the Farmers Union.

6. If the official poverty level were adjusted to include food stamps and housing vouchers it would
   a. significantly increase the number of people classified as living below the poverty line.
   b. dramatically lower the percentage of the population below the poverty line.
   c. only marginally lower the percentage of the population above the poverty line.
   d. effectively reduce the level of benefits.

7. The Welfare Reform bill of 1996 gave more control over welfare to
   a. the national government.
   b. state governments.
   c. local government.
   d. the private sector.

8. During the first 5 years of welfare reform, families receiving benefits declined by
   a. 20 percent.
   b. 30 percent
   c. 40 percent
   d. 50 percent

9. The fastest-growing subgroup of the homeless population is
   a. street people.
   b. the mentally ill.
   c. illegal immigrants.
   d. families.

10. The National Environmental Policy Act created the
    a. environmental impact statements
    b. Clean Air Act.
    c. Ozone limits.
    d. Clean Water Act

11. In recent years, serious crimes committed by _____ significantly increased.
    a. women
    b. juveniles
    c. immigrants
    d. the elderly

12. The majority of arrests today involve
    a. murder.
    b. drug offenses.
    c. federal crimes.
    d. white collar crimes.

13. Legal methods in the tax code for avoiding taxes are referred to as
    a. justifications.
    b. hidden benefits.
    c. loopholes.
    d. give-backs.

14. Policies regulating the amount of money in circulation are part of a
    a. fiscal policy
    b. national economizing
    c. monetary policy
    d. zero sum budgeting

15. Monetary policy is primarily made by the
    a. President
    b. Congress
    c. Federal Reserve
    d. Treasury Secretary

16. Public Debt can be defined as
    a. the limit on how much money Congress can spend.
    b. the yearly amount of money owed by the government
    c. the total amount of money owed by the government
    d. the amount of money owed for Wartime expenditures

17. The adoption of a common currency should benefit the economy of
    a. Mexico
    b. Japan
    c. China
    d. European Union

18. The deficit spending, which occurred after the terrorist attack, was inflated with spending on
    a. corporate retirement
    b. educational grants
    c. farm subsidy spending
    d. welfare benefit increases

19. The use of fiscal policy to alter economic variables is the underlying premise for
    a. supply and demand.
    b. Keynesian economics.
    c. Marxist economic theory.
    d. the global economy.

20. Monetary policy does not suffer from the same lengthy time lags as fiscal policy does, because
    a. monetary policy does not have an immediate effect upon consumers.
    b. the president can act more quickly than Congress to implement monetary policy.
    c. The Federal Reserve can, within a very short time, put its policy into effect.
    d. Congress can act quickly when needed to solve economic problems.

Short Essay Questions. Briefly address the major concepts raised by the following questions.

1. Explain and discuss the steps in the policymaking process.

2. Discuss the major provisions of the Welfare Reform Act of 1996. What impact will this act have on the poor in America?

3. Analyze the issues of crime in the United States.

4. Discuss the major laws attempting to protect the nation's environment.

ANSWERS TO THE PRACTICE EXAM

Fill-in-the-Blank.

1.	domestic policy	[p. 485]
2.	agenda adoption	[p. 486]
3.	aviation security	[p. 485]
4.	income transfers	[p. 487]
5.	years	[p. 491]
6.	juveniles	[p. 492]
7.	drug offenses	[p. 493]
8.	American Revolution	[p. 495]
9.	National Environmental Policy Act	[p. 496]
10.	loopholes	[p. 499]

True/False.

1.	T	[p. 485]	3.	T	[p. 488]	5.	F	[p. 490]	7.	T	[p. 497]	9.	T	[p. 497]
2.	T	[p. 487]	4.	F	[p. 489]	6.	T	[p. 492]	8.	F	[p. 495]	10.	F	[p. 506]

Multiple-Choice.

1.	c	[p. 485]	6.	b	[p. 488]	11. b	[p. 492]	16. c	[p. 505]
2.	b	[p. 486]	7.	b	[p. 489]	12. b	[p. 493]	17. d	[p. 506]
3.	d	[p. 487]	8.	d	[p. 489]	13. c	[p. 499]	18. c	[p. 507]
4.	b	[p. 487]	9.	d	[p. 491]	14. c	[p. 503]	19. b	[p. 504]
5.	b	[p. 488]	10.	a	[p. 496]	15. c	[p. 504]	20. c	[p. 505]

Short Essay Answers

1. Explain and discuss the steps in the policy-making process [p. 485-487]. The policymaking process contains five major steps.
   - Agenda building is the first step of recognition of a problem. The media, strong personalities, and interest groups usually facilitate this step.
   - Agenda formulation is the discussion between the government and the public of various proposals to solve the problem. .
   - Agenda adoption is the selection by Congress of a specific strategy from the proposals, which were discussed.
   - Agenda implementation is the government action implemented by bureaucrats, the courts, police, and individual citizens.
   - Agenda evaluation is groups inside and outside receiving "feedback" about the policy.

2. Discuss the major laws attempting to protect the nation's environment [p. 495-498].

   - Government legislation to control pollution can be traced back before the American Revolution. See Table 16-3, page 539 for major federal environmental legislation.
   - The most concerted effort to clean up the environment begins in 1969 with the passage of the National Environmental Policy Act. This law provides for an environmental impact statement (EIS) to be prepared for all major federal actions that may impact the environment.
   - The 1990 Clean Air Act was designed to clean up air pollution. A major environmental problem of air pollution was acid rain.
   - The costs of cleaning up the environment have become a major political issue beginning in the 1990s.

3. Identify the difference between fiscal policy and monetary policy [p. 503-505].
   - Fiscal policy is the change in government spending or taxation to alter national economic variables.
   - Fiscal policy is under the control of Congress and the president.
   - In a recession, which is a period of rising unemployment, the government will stimulate the economy by increasing government expenditures and by decreasing taxes. During inflation, which is rapid increases in employment and rising prices, the government will "cool off" the economy by reducing expenditures and increasing taxes.
   - Monetary policy is the change in the amount of money in circulation to alter national economic variables.
   - Monetary policy is under the control of the Federal Reserve System, or the Fed.

- In a recession, the Fed will stimulate the economy by expanding the rate of growth of the money supply. During inflation, the Fed will "cool off" the economy by reducing the rate of growth of the amount of money in circulation.

4. Identify the differences between the federal deficit and the national debt. How does the government deal with national debt? [p. 505-506]
   - The federal deficit occurs when the federal government spends more money in a year than it receives. From 1960 to 1998, the federal government usually operated at a deficit.
   - The national debt is the total amount of debt carried by the federal government from all yearly deficits.
   - Public debt financing is a process of issuing or selling U.S. Treasury bonds. The government can never go bankrupt, as long as it can make interest payments.
   - Public debt financing can affect the economy by "crowding out" private borrowing.
   - The federal deficit was ended in 1998 but reappeared in 2001.

Chapter 17
FOREIGN AND DEFENSE POLICY

CHAPTER SUMMARY

Facing the World: Foreign and Defense Policy?

Foreign policy is a nation's external goals and the techniques and strategies used to achieve them. Two key aspects of foreign policy are national security—the protection of the independence and political integrity of the United States, and diplomacy, the settlement of disputes and conflicts among nations by peaceful methods [p. 515-516].

Morality versus Reality in Foreign Policy

From the beginning of the United States, Americans have felt a special destiny to provide moral leadership to the rest of the world. Many of the U.S. foreign policy initiatives seem to be rooted in moral idealism. This philosophy sees all nations as willing to cooperate and agree on moral standards for conduct. The Peace Corps, established by President Kennedy, is a good example of this concept. In opposition to the moral perspective is political realism. This philosophy sees the world as a dangerous place in which each nation strives for survival. The United States has generally pursued a foreign policy that attempts to balance these philosophies [p. 516-517].

Challenges in World Politics

In a new development, dissident groups, rebels, and other revolutionaries have used modern weapons to engage in terrorism in order to affect world politics. The long-standing regional conflict in the Middle East has produced a number of terrorist acts worldwide in the last two decades. In 2001, terrorism came to the United States with the attacks on the World Trade Center and Pentagon. The dissolution of the Soviet Union brought a lowering of tensions among the nuclear powers, but the number and location of nuclear weapons continues to be a major problem. The emergence of China, as a major trading partner of the United States and the most populous nation in the world, has altered world trade policies. This is just one of the major developments of the Global economy. Since the 1980s, the United States has become a debtor nation. We owe more to foreigners than foreigners owe to us. Regional conflicts all over the globe have replaced the Cold War as a major focus of U.S. foreign policy. Unrest in the island nations of Haiti and Cuba produced a flood of immigration, which has particularly affected the state of Florida. Conflict in the Middle East, between Israel and its Arab neighbors, has been a concern of the United States since the conflict began in 1948. In a related mid-east issue, the United States sent more than a half-million troops to push Iraq out of Kuwait in 1991. The collapse of the former Yugoslavia in Eastern Europe required the intervention of the United States and European nations to prevent the Serbs from killing ethnic groups. Ethnic violence in Africa also flared in the 1990s. The United States has played little role in these conflicts, except for a limited effort to bring humanitarian aid to Somalia in 1992-1995. In recent years, violence in Africa has been made worse by a wide spread AIDS epidemic. [p. 518-529].

Who Makes Foreign Policy?

While the President has important foreign policy powers, the Constitution gives Congress the opportunity to review these powers. The two most significant presidential powers are the negotiation of treaties and leadership of the armed forces as commander-in-chief. But Congress has the authority to declare war, and the Senate must ratify treaties by a two-thirds vote. Presidents have used the executive agreements to get around the requirement of Senate-approved treaties. Finally, the Constitution gives the President the right to appoint ambassadors and recognize foreign governments. The president also has informal powers in the foreign policy process. These powers are his access to intelligence from the CIA and military, his ability to influence budget priorities, and his influence on public opinion. In addition to the president, there are at least four foreign policymaking sources within the executive branch. These are:

- the Department of State, the executive agency most directly engaged in day-to-day foreign policy
- the National Security Council, responsible for advising the president on domestic, foreign, and military policies affecting national security

- the intelligence community composed of all government agencies involved in intelligence activities. See page 532 for a list of the most important intelligence agencies.
- the Department of Defense, which brings all military agencies under one organization [p. 529-533]

Congress Balances the President

The struggle between the president and Congress over foreign policy questions reached a highpoint during the Vietnam War (1964-1975). In 1973, Congress passed, over President's Nixon's veto, the War Powers Resolution. This law required the president to "consult" with Congress before using troops in military action. Congress has also been more cautious in supporting the president where military involvement of American troops is possible. This has restored some of the balance of the relationship of the president and Congress in foreign policy [p. 533].

Domestic Sources of Foreign Policy

Besides the president and Congress, foreign policy is also influenced by sources in society, which include elite and mass opinion, and the military-industrial complex. Public opinion of the attentive public—that portion of the general public that pays attention to foreign policy issues—is particularly important. This segment represents about 10 to 20 percent of all citizens. The military-industrial complex, which President Eisenhower warned the nation about, is the mutually beneficial relationship between the armed forces and defense contractors [p. 533-534].

The Major Foreign Policy Themes

An historical review of American foreign policy reveals several major themes. In the early days of our nation, the founding fathers held a basic mistrust of alliances with European nations. The Monroe doctrine of 1823 set forth a U.S. policy of isolationism toward Europe, a policy characterized by abstaining from an active role in international affairs or alliances, particularly with Europe. The end of the isolationist policy started with the Spanish-American War in 1898, and continued through World War I (1914-1918). This policy is generally called interventionism. After World War I, America returned to a policy of isolationism. World War II shattered isolationism forever, with the Japanese attack on Pearl Harbor, Hawaii on December 7, 1941. This event ushered in the period of internationalism in American foreign policy, which continues today. The United States and the Soviet Union were wartime allies against Adolph Hitler's Germany. After the war, the alliance fell apart, and the United States and the Soviet Union, in a Cold War, began a 50-year struggle for supremacy. The Soviet Union seized Eastern Europe and divided Europe by what Winston Churchill called an "iron curtain." The United States adopted a policy of containment by a series of encircling military alliances to prevent the spread of communist government. The military alliances were tests in a series of military actions, usually by "client" nations of each side. In the Korean War (1950-1953), and the Vietnam War (1964-1975), the United States engaged directly in military action. The Cuban Missile Crisis in 1962 brought the world to the brink of nuclear war, but after this crisis was peacefully negotiated, the United States, and the Soviet Union began a period of relaxed tension called détente. The Strategic Arms Limitation Treaty (SALT) began a process of reducing nuclear weapons. President Reagan's hardstand with the Soviet Union recalled the early days of the Cold War. Reagan's proposal for an expensive, space-based, missile defense system led to the collapse of the Soviet economy and the end of the Cold War [p. 534-541].

Foreign and Defense Policy: Why Is It Important Today?

The end of the Cold War has altered the needs of the U.S. military to protect the security of the United States. Regional conflicts will continue to require a more flexible military force. The terrorist attacks on September 11, 2001 emphasized the importance of foreign policy to domestic security. The United States will need to cooperate with organizations like the United Nations to work with other nations to resolve conflicts. The global economy and global issues will become more important to the United States in the next century [p. 541].

KEY TERMS

attentive public—p. 534
cold war—p. 537
containment—p. 537
détente—p. 539
foreign policy—p. 515
intelligence community—p. 532
iron curtain—p. 537
isolationist foreign policy—p. 535

military-industrial complex—p. 534
Monroe Doctrine—p. 535
moral idealism—p. 516
National Security Council (NSC) —p. 516
political realism—p. 517
Strategic Arms Limitation
Treaty (SALT I) —p. 539

OTHER RESOURCES

A number of valuable supplements are available to students using the Schmidt, Shelley, and Bardes text. The full list of the supplements is in the preface to this study guide. Ask your instructor how to obtain these resources. One supplement is highlighted here, the INFOTRAC Online Library.

INFOTRAC EXERCISES

Log on to http://www.infotrac-college.com.
Enter your Pass code that came with your textbook.
You can access the article by typing the exact phrase below.

Isoleteralism or Unilationism?
The premise of this article is that the rejection of the Comprehensive Test Ban Treaty by the Senate in 1999 has created a new foreign policy model, which combines Isolationism and Unilateralism. The U.S. is acting in isolation in foreign affairs instead of being in isolation.

Study Questions
1. What is the concept of Isolation?
2. What is the concept of Unilateralsim?
3. How do these concepts fit the foreign policy of George W. Bush?

Code Red: Internet Security
The premise of this article is the National Security Council's Critical Infrastructure Assurance Office (CIAO) is working with industry groups to prevent cyberspace attacks.

Study Questions
1. What specific areas of security on the Internet are referred to in the article?
2. Do you think the September 11 attack had an impact on this issue?
3. Do think the government should police the Internet?

Managing domestic and foreign Policies
The premise of this article is that since WW II, Presidents have had much greater success in foreign policy issues than in domestic policy.

Study Questions
1. What has been the presidential success rate on domestic and foreign policy?
2. What are the reasons that presidents are more successful in foreign policy?
3. Who are the presidents competitors for control of foreign policy?

Haiti Puts Hex
The premise of this article is that the United States has spend $3 billion dollars in program assistance to Haiti without much to show for the spending.

Study Questions

1. What are the reasons for so much program assistance to Haiti?
2. Why was the United States involved in elections in Haiti?
3. Why does the United States continue to have concerns about Haiti?

PRACTICE EXAM
(Answers appear at the end of this chapter.)

Fill-in-the-Blank. Supply the missing word(s) or term(s) to complete the sentence.

1. _____ _____ describes U.S. goals, techniques, and strategies in the world arena.

2. _____ refers to the peaceful settlement of disputes and conflicts among nations.

3. The _____ _____ is the executive agency most directly engaged in foreign affairs.

4. The _____ _____ formed the basis for the U.S. foreign policy of isolationism.

5. The lasting change in American foreign policy came with the end of _____ _____ _____.

6.. The George F. Kennan doctrine, which became the bible of western foreign policy, was _____.

7. President Eisenhower warned the nation about the influence of the _____ _____ _____.

8. The French word that means a relaxation of tensions is _____.

9. The United States currently imports more goods and services than it exports; it has a

_____ _____.

10. China sought and was granted _____ _____ _____ _____ for tariffs and trade by the U.S.

True/False. Circle the appropriate letter to indicate if the statement is true or false.

T   F   1. National security policy concerns itself with the defense of the U.S. against actual or potential enemies.

T   F   2. Diplomacy is the set of negotiation techniques by which the U.S. attempts to carry out its foreign policy.

T   F   3. The Peace Corps is a good example of America's moral idealism in practice.

T   F   4. Political realism has always been the only guiding principle in foreign policy decisions for the U.S.

T	F	5.	China has become a major trading partner of the United States.
T	F	6.	The State Department's preeminence in foreign policy has gradually increased since WW II.
T	F	7.	The attentive public seems to be less interested in foreign policy than domestic policy.
T	F	8.	U.S. foreign policy during its formative years could be described as interventionist.
T	F	9.	The Star Wars policy of President Clinton brought an end to the Communist threat.
T	F	10.	The Truman Doctrine is a clear expression of the U.S. policy of containment.

Multiple-Choice. Circle the correct response.

1. Diplomacy differs from foreign policy in that
   a. diplomacy is a set of techniques and strategies used to achieve a foreign policy goal.
   b. diplomacy is the all encompassing goal while foreign policy is a sub-set.
   c. the president develops diplomacy and the State Department develops foreign policy.
   d. diplomacy always comes first followed by a specific foreign policy.

2. Foreign policy based on moral imperatives is often unsuccessful for the U.S. because it
   a. makes policy making difficult to understand.
   b. assumes that other nations agree with American views of morality and politics.
   c. requires the president to establish absolute standards of conduct for U.S. personnel.
   d. makes too many enemies.

3. The foreign policy that allows the U.S. to sell weapons to dictators who support American business interests around the world, and to repel terrorism with force is the policy of
   a. détente.
   b. moral idealism.
   c. counterintelligence.
   d. political realism.

4. Edwin S. Corwin observed that the Constitution creates an "invitation to struggle" between the president and Congress for control over
   a. economic policy.
   b. appointments to the Supreme Court.
   c. foreign aid.
   d. the foreign policy process.

5. Since the Second World War almost 95% understandings reached between the United States and other nations have come in the form of
   a. protocols.
   b. legislative mandates.
   c. executive agreements.
   d. treaties.

6. The making of foreign policy is often viewed as a presidential prerogative because
   a. as opposed to making domestic policy, most presidents enjoy making foreign policy.
   b. of the president's constitutional power in this area and the resources of the executive branch.
   c. the Constitution clearly denies Congress a role in formulating foreign policy.
   d. the War Powers Act delegated this authority to the president.

7. The major provision of the War Powers Act was to
    a. limit the president's use of troops in military action without congressional approval.
    b. allow the president more freedom in the use of military troops throughout the world.
    c. give the president new powers in the area of foreign policy.
    d. prevent aggressor nations from becoming too strong militarily.

8. Generally, the efforts of the president and the elites to influence foreign policy are most successful with that segment of the population called the
    a. zealots.
    b. mass public.
    c. attentive public.
    d. thoughtful public.

9. The Monroe Doctrine states that the U.S.
    a. had territorial dominion over South America.
    b. was neutral in its relations with Europe and Asia.
    c. could trade openly with China.
    d. would not meddle in European internal affairs and would not accept foreign intervention in the Western Hemisphere.

10. The strategic defense initiative (SDI or Star Wars) was proposed as a program that would deter nuclear war by
    a. shifting the emphasis of defense strategy from offensive to defensive weapons systems.
    b. shifting our defense to an offensive weapons system.
    c. developing more intercontinental ballistic missiles.
    d. allowing for joint United States/Soviet Union development of manned space stations with laser guided missiles for world domination.

11. The event that signified the Soviet Union had relinquished its political and military control over the states of Eastern Europe was the
    a. renewed interest in Cuba.
    b. fall of the Berlin Wall.
    c. defeat in Afghanistan.
    d. dissolution of the Soviet Union.

12. The end of the Cold War means that U.S. foreign policy will need to be
    a. much more stable and predictable than it has been before.
    b. directed at policing the world because the U.S. is the only superpower today.
    c. basically directed at economic aid to underdeveloped countries.
    d. much more flexible in order to deal with changing conditions and complex situations.

13. Operation Desert Storm carried out by the U.S. and a coalition of other nations lead to the
    a. overthrow of Saddam Hussein in Iraq.
    b. overthrow of the Sheikdom of Kuwait.
    c. restoration of the Sheikdom of Kuwait.
    d. overthrow of the government in Iran.

14. The Helms-Burton Act created an embargo, which remains today, against the nation of
    a. Haiti.
    b. Cuba.
    c. Iraq.
    d. Iran.

15. Concern over nuclear weapon proliferation intensified in 1999, when the Senate rejected the
    a. China/North Korea Treaty.
    b. Comprehensive Nuclear Test Ban Treaty.
    c. Middle East Peace Treaty.
    d. Nuclear Terrorism Treaty.

16. Which of the following is NOT an informal technique of the president to influence foreign policy?
    a. his access to information
    b. his ability to influence public opinion
    c. his ability to influence government spending
    d. his ability to recognize foreign governments

17. The role of the National Security Council is to
    a. shape executive agreements for the president.
    b. protect the president overseas.
    c. advise the president on the integration of policies relating to national security.
    d. supervise the CIA.

18. The president who warned the nation of the influence of the military-industrial complex was
    a. Eisenhower.
    b. Nixon.
    c. Reagan.
    d. Clinton.

19. The START treaty
    a. allowed Russia to join NATO.
    b. reduced the number of long-range nuclear weapons.
    c. gave China most-favored-nation status.
    d. created the "Star Wars" initiative.

20. Tensions between the U.S. and Cuba increased tremendously in 1999-2000 because of the
    a. Cuban Missile Crisis.
    b. embargo of Cuba by the U.S.
    c. status of Elian Gonzales.
    d. Cuban takeover of Guantanamo Naval Base.

Short Essay Questions. Briefly address the major concepts raised by the following questions.

1. Describe the formal and informal powers of the president to make foreign policy.

2. Trace the stages of United States foreign policy development from isolationism through détente.

3. Discuss the current foreign policy challenges the U.S. faces today, besides regional conflicts.

4. Summarize the role that the U.S. has played in recent regional conflicts.

ANSWERS TO THE PRACTICE EXAM

Fill-in-the-Blank

1. Foreign policy   [p. 515]
2. Diplomacy   [p. 516]
3. State Department   [p. 531]
4. Monroe Doctrine   [p. 535]
5. World War II   [p. 536]
6. containment   [p. 537]
7. military-industrial complex   [p. 534]
8. détente   [p. 539]
9. trade deficit   [p. 523]
10. most-favored-nation status   [p. 522]

True/False

1. T [p. 515]   3. T [p. 517]   5. T [p. 522]   7. F [p. 534]   9. F [p. 540]
2. T [p. 516]   4. F [p. 517]   6. F [p. 531]   8. F [p. 535]   10. T [p. 537]

Multiple Choice

1. a [p. 516]   6. b [p. 530]   11. b [p. 540]   16. d [p. 530]
2. b [p. 517]   7. a [p. 533]   12. d [p. 541]   17. c [p. 531]
3. d [p. 517]   8. c [p. 534]   13. c [p. 525]   18. a [p. 534]
4. d [p. 529]   9. d [p. 535]   14. b [p. 525]   19. b [p. 540]
5. c [p. 530]   10. a [p. 540]   15. b [p. 520]   20. c [p. 525]

Short Essay Answers. An adequate short answer consists of several paragraphs that discuss the concepts addressed by the question. Always demonstrate your knowledge of the ideas by giving examples. The following represent the major ideas that should be included in these short essays.

1. Describe the formal and informal powers of the president to make foreign policy [p. 529-531].

    *   The Constitution provides the president with two main areas of foreign policy authority:
        *   Article II, Section 1 designates the president as Commander-in-Chief of the armed forces.
        *   Article II, Section 2 gives the president the power to make treaties with the consent of two-thirds of the Senate.
        *   Additional foreign policy power is granted to appoint ambassadors, other public ministers, and consuls. Section 3 gives the president the power to recognize foreign governments.
    *   The informal powers of the president to conduct foreign policy are his superior access to information, his ability to lobby Congress for funds, his influence over public opinion, and his head-of-state moral leadership position to commit the United States to a course of action.

2. Trace the stages of United States foreign policy from isolationism through détente [p. 534-539].

    *   The founders of the United States distrusted the European nations, and attempted to stay out of European conflicts and politics. This policy of isolation from Europe was stated in the Monroe Doctrine in 1823.
    *   The end of the isolationist policy started with the Spanish-American War in 1898. It continued to change in World War I when the United States intervened in a European conflict.
    *   Isolation returned after World War I in reaction to that conflict.

- Isolation ended forever on December 7, 1941, when the Japanese attacked Pearl Harbor, Hawaii, and the United States was thrust into World War II. The era of Internationalism had begun.
- Although the United States and the Soviet Union were wartime allies against Nazi Germany, the alliance quickly fell apart after the war. The Soviet Union wanted a divided Germany, and seized control of Eastern Europe to create a Soviet Bloc, which would challenge the Western world in an ideological, political, and economic struggle known as the Cold War.
- The United States foreign policy throughout the cold War was called "containment" of the spread of Communist nations. This was well stated in the Truman Doctrine: to halt Communist expansion in southeastern Europe.
- In the Cuban Missile Crisis of 1962, the United States and the Soviet Union confronted each other over the placement of Soviet missiles in Cuba. This crisis led the world to the brink of a nuclear World War III. After intense negotiations, the crisis was resolved in a peaceful manner.
- After the Cuban Missile Crisis, the United States and the Soviet Union realized that they had to reduce the threat of nuclear war. Under the leadership of President Nixon and Henry Kissinger, a period of détente, or relaxation of tensions, began. The first tangible result of détente was the Strategic Arms Limitation Treaty (SALT I) signed in 1972.

3. Discuss the current foreign policy challenges the U.S. faces, besides regional conflicts [p. 517-523].

- Terrorism has become both a domestic and foreign policy problem for the United States. The act of September 11, 2001 has brought terrorism to the United States. Much terrorism has stemmed from the Middle East crisis between Israel and the Arab nations.
- Nuclear proliferation remains a world problem as more nations join the "Nuclear Club."
- President Nixon was responsible for opening diplomatic and economic relationships with Communist China in the 1970s. China has become a major trading partner of the United States in the 1990s. China sought and received most-favored-nation status for tariffs and trade policy from the United States. In 1997, China took control of Hong Kong from the British, and has preserved the free enterprise system.
- The global economy has created an interdependent world, in which the events of one region can affect the entire world. The political structures of the nation states, perhaps under the United Nations, must adapt and change to deal with the world of the twenty-first century.

4. Summarize the role that the U.S. has played in recent regional conflicts [p. 524-529

- The island nations of Haiti and Cuba have had a major impact on domestic as well as foreign policy issues for the U.S. Immigrants from both countries flooded into Florida. Continuing problems with the communist government in Cuba led the United States to pass the Helms-Burton Act for an embargo of Cuba.
- The Middle East crisis between Israel and its Arab neighbors has been a long-standing regional conflict. The United States has repeatedly tried to bring about a peaceful settlement of the conflict.
- The invasion of Kuwait by Iraq in 1990 has created an additional Middle East crisis for the U.S. In Operation Desert Storm, the United States, with a coalition of nations under United Nations authority, pushed Iraq out of Kuwait. Iraq, under United Nations sanctions, has continued to defy the world and created an environment of regional tension.
- The breakup of the Soviet Union lead to profound change in Eastern Europe. The former nation of Yugoslavia broke into a number of nations, which were engulfed in war with Serbia, the dominant part of Yugoslavia. This war continues today, as the United States and other European nations seek a peaceful solution to the conflict.
- Ethnic conflicts have broken out in a number of African nations. The conflicts have been made more devastating because of drought, AIDS, and famine conditions in many countries. The efforts of the United Nations and United States have been unable to stop the conflicts.

Chapter 18
STATE AND LOCAL GOVERNMENT

CHAPTER SUMMARY

The U. S. Constitution and the State Governments

The U.S. governmental system is one national government and fifty separate state governments. The U.S. Constitution reserves power to the states:

- The states may take any action not prohibited by the Constitution or given expressly and exclusively to the national government.
- States can tax, spend, and regulate intrastate commerce.
- States also have general police power to promote and safeguard the health, morals, safety, and welfare of the people [p. 551-552].

State Constitutions

State constitutions are usually long and detailed, an aspect that can be traced to the loss of popular confidence in state legislatures between the end of the Civil War and the early 1900s. In addition, framers of state constitution may have felt it necessary to fill in the gaps of the very brief U.S. Constitution. Changes to state constitutions are usually carried out by constitutional conventions. Eighteen states, such as California and Oregon, allow for a constitutional initiative, which provides for citizens to petition placing proposed constitution amendments directly on the ballot [p. 552-553].

The State Executive Branch

The tradition of powerful colonial governors in our early history has lead many states to weaken the power of state governors. The influence of Jacksonian democracy has created a large number of independently elected executive figures in addition to the governor. The election of so many officials tends to fragment executive authority, and many states have tried to strengthen the power of their governor. A state governorship is a stepping-stone to the presidency as seventeen presidents have served as state governors before becoming president. In 43 states state governors hold the important power of line item veto on appropriations. Congress tried to give this power to the president, but the Supreme Court of the U.S. ruled the law unconstitutional. [p. 553-556].

The State Legislature

State legislatures have often been criticized for being unprofessional and ineffective. State legislators are often given few resources to accomplish their functions, as states limit salaries and the time the legislature can meet. In eight states, including Texas, legislators are paid less than $10,000 per year. See Table 18-1, p. 557, for the characteristics of state legislatures, including salaries. One of the major functions of state legislatures is to reapportion both state and federal legislative districts every ten years after the federal census. Gerrymandering, in which the majority party manipulates reapportionment for its own benefit, continues to be a problem. Many state legislatures have provided for more citizen input by initiative, referendum, and recall. Under these provisions, which do not exist at the national level, citizens can directly propose constitutional, and legislative changes, and remove officials from office. See figure 18-1, p. 558 for how an idea becomes a law. [p. 556-560].

The State Judiciary

Each state, including the District of Columbia, has its own court system. See Figure 18-2, p. 562, for a view of a sample state court system. State judges can either be elected or appointed depending upon the level of the court and the state. State courts, which handle the bulk of cases in the United States, have severe problems of under funding and overwork [p. 560-562].

How Local Government Operates

The U.S. Constitution makes no mention of local government. The state creates every local government. In 1811, Dillon's rule established the very narrow interpretation that local government could only possess the powers specifically given it by the state. The home-rule-for-cities movement against state control culminated in Cooley's rule, which advocated that cities govern themselves. Since 1900, most states allow home-rule cities to write their own city charters and govern themselves within state laws. The four major types of local governmental units are municipalities or cities, counties, towns and townships, and special districts. See Table 18-2, p. 565 for the numbers and types of local governments in the U.S.

With over eighty thousand local governments in the United States, the trend toward consolidation of two or more government units into a single unit, is understandable. The most successful form of consolidation has been functional consolidation, which focuses on cooperation to provide services to inhabitants in that area. The federal government has encouraged the use of a council of government (COG) to focus on area wide problems. The structure of governing cities or municipalities can be divided into four general types:

- the commission plan—developed in Galveston, Texas, and combined legislative and executive power in the hands of a small group of individuals
- the council-manager plan—centers the executive power in the hands of a professional city manager hired by the city council to run the city
- the mayor-administrator plan—used in big cities, where the mayor is chief executive but appoints an administration to do routine administrative tasks
- the mayor-council plan—the mayor is the chief executive officer. The amount of power the mayor has depends or whether it is a weak or strong mayor form of government.

For much of the late nineteenth and early twentieth centuries, major cities were run by political "machines." These were usually strong mayors who used patronage to get elected and reelected. Reforms developed, including other structures of city government, such as council manager. Political machines were replaced, but they were generally much more effective in providing access to government services for economically disadvantaged city residents. Large cities have struggled to try to provide services for more and more people. Cities have tried governing the metro area as a whole, annexing suburbs, consolidating local government functions, and creating special metropolitan districts to provide specific services. [563-570]

Paying for State and Local Government

State and local government provide the bulk of spending for education in this nation. See Table 18-3, p. 570, for state expenditures, and Table 18-4 for local expenditures. The most important tax at the state level is the general sales tax. The major revenue source for local government is the property tax. In the 1980, many state budgets doubled as the federal government cut back on its aid to states. State governments tried two approaches to maintain balanced budgets. One was to increase taxes, and the other was to reduce spending. The states that reduced spending generally had better economies, and a number of states experienced budget surpluses [p. 570-573].

State and Local Government: Why Is It Important Today?

The federal government continues to give states more responsibility to solve more problems. States appear likely to give local governments more responsibility to deal with crime, pollution, and congestion. State and local governments will continue to face the challenge of providing our children with a world class education and finding the resources to pay for this education [p. 573].

KEY TERMS

charter—p. 563
consolidation—p. 565
constitutional initiative—p. 553
Cooley's Rule—p. 563
Council of government (COG)—p. 566
county—p. 564
Dillon's Rule—p. 563

general law city—p. 563
general sales tax—p. 572
home rule city—p. 563
municipal home rule —p. 563
patronage—p. 568
police power—p. 551
property tax—p. 572
referendum—p. 559

OTHER RESOURCES

A number of valuable supplements are available to students using the Schmidt, Shelley, and Bardes text. The full list of the supplements is in the preface to this study guide. Ask your instructor how to obtain these resources. One supplement is highlighted here, the INFOTRAC Online Library.

INFOTRAC EXERCISES

Log on to http://www.infotrac-college.com.
Enter your Pass code that came with your textbook.
Use the CD that came with your textbook for suggestions for articles in this chapter.

PRACTICE EXAM
(Answers appear at the end of this chapter.)

Fill-in-the-Blank. Supply the missing word(s) or term(s) to complete the sentence.

1. The recall and initiative are examples of _____ _____, in which the people vote directly on important issues.

2. Each of the fifty states, as well as the District of Columbia, has it own separate _____ system.

3. The view that cities should be able to govern themselves is called _____ _____.

4. The most successful forms of government consolidations have been _____ consolidations.

5. The _____ lets citizens bypass legislatures and propose new statutes in government.

6. A voluntary organization of counties and municipalities concerned with areawide problems is the _____ _____ _____.

7. The _____ form of municipal government is the oldest and most widely used.

8. Rewarding faithful party workers and followers with jobs is called _____.

9. By far the most important tax at the state level is the _____ _____ _____ and at the local level, the _____ _____.

10. _____ is the biggest category of expenditure at the local level of government.

True/False. Circle the appropriate letter to indicate if the statement is true or false.

T F 1. The U.S. has more than eighty-thousand separate local governmental units.

T F 2. Compared to the U.S. Constitution, state constitutions are surprisingly brief and rather general documents.

T F 3. Most states follow the practice of electing numerous executive officials.

T F 4. The states hold general police powers to protect the health, morals, and safety of their citizens.

T F 5. Local government are considered to be creatures of the state government without independent status of their own.

T F 6. County governments are extremely complex entities, a product of Jacksonian democracy.

T F 7. The most numerous form of local government is the special district.

T F 8. The major defect of the council-manager form of government is that there is no single, strong political executive leader.

T F 9. By far the most important tax at the state level is the personal income tax.

T F 10. Today, states have been successful in reducing their budget deficits by increasing state taxes.

Multiple-Choice. Circle the correct response.

1. The major reserved powers of the states are the powers to
    a. regulate health care, transportation, and education.
    b. control education, build highways, and provide for the general welfare.
    c. tax, spend, and regulate intrastate commerce.
    c. control the election process, charter banks, and coin money.

2. One of the important tenets of Jacksonian democracy was
    a. the fewer public officials elected, the better the quality of decision-making.
    b. that public employees should be selected on merit, not partisanship.
    c. the more public officials elected, the more democratic the system.
    d. that the national government should be supreme in all spheres of life.

3. According to historians, the length and mass of detail of many state constitutions reflects a(n)
    a. interest in clarifying the public good.
    b. loss of popular confidence in state legislatures between the end of the Civil War and early 1900s.
    c. high esteem for state government by the framers of state constitutions.
    d. a desire that state constitutions serve as clear guides to future decision-makers.

4. Many governors have the power of the item veto, which they use on legislation called
    a. authorization bills.
    b. appropriation bills.
    c. general welfare bills.
    d. constitutional amendments.

5. The initiative, referendum, and recall all represent forms of
    a. representative democracy.
    b. indirect democracy.
    c. minority rule.
    d. direct democracy.

6. The procedure enabling voters to remove an elected official from office before his term has expired is
    a. recall.
    b. recommit.
    c. impeachment process.
    d. referendum.

7. Dillon's Rule states that
    a. local governments can perform any function they choose unless forbidden by state law.
    b. state government can create local government at their own choosing.
    c. local governments can exercise only those powers expressly given or fairly implied by the state.
    d. local government derives its power from the fourteenth amendment of the U.S. Constitution.

8. The difference between a county and a municipality is that a county
    a. may not be created at the behest of its inhabitants.
    b. is always geographically larger than a municipality.
    c. can determine its own form of government.
    d. performs more important service than a municipality.

9. The union of two or more governmental units to form a single unit is referred to as a
    a. federation.
    b. unionization.
    c. consolidation.
    d. merging.

10. Local government units have addressed regional problems primarily through the organization of
    a. interstate compacts.
    b. metropolitan federation.
    c. special districts.
    d. council of government.

11. The form of municipal government that combines both executive and legislative powers in the hands of the same elected members is referred to as the
    a. mayor-council plan.
    b. commission plan.
    c. council-manager plan.
    d. mayor-administrator plan.

12. The form of municipal government that appoints an administrative officer to do routine tasks is the
    a. council-manager plan.
    b. commission plan.
    c. mayor-council plan.
    d. mayor-administrator plan.

13. Which of the following techniques helps to deal with the loss of tax base in large cities?
    a. hiring a city manager.
    b. using the commission form of city government.
    c. annexation of surrounding areas.
    d. developing a suburban growth plan.

14. The biggest category of expenditure for state and local governments is
    a. police protection.
    b. health.
    c. public welfare.
    d. education.

15. The major source of tax revenues at the local level is
    a. franchise taxes.
    b. general sales tax.
    c. property taxes.
    d. personal income taxes.

16. The most important tax at the state level of government is
    a. personal income tax
    b. property tax
    c. general sales tax
    d. franchise taxes

17. The number of states, which rely on personal income taxes as a revenue source is
    a. under 10
    b. about half (25)
    c. around 35
    d. all 50

18. One of the new revenue source adopted by three-fourth of the states is
    a. personal income tax
    b. state lottery
    c. profit operated state businesses
    d. profits from stock market investments

19. The average amount of federal government aid to state government is
    a. 10 percent
    b. 20 percent
    c. 30 percent
    d. 40 percent

20. Cutbacks of state funding in the 21st century have resulted in less funding to
    a. highway funds
    b. police and security
    c. legislator's salaries
    d. education

Short Essay Questions. Briefly address the major concepts raised by the following questions.

1. Discuss the provisions of direct democracy that many states allow in their constitution.

2. Explain the four major types of local government units.

3. Discuss the four general plans for governing municipalities.

4. Examine the basic areas of revenues and expenditures for state and local government.

ANSWERS TO THE PRACTICE EXAM

Fill-in-the-Blank.

1. direct democracy   [p. 559]
2. court   [p. 560]
3. Cooley's Rule   [p. 563]
4. functional   [p. 566]
5. initiative   [p. 559]
6. Council of Government   [p. 566]
7. mayor-council   [p. 568]
8. patronage   [p. 568]
9. general sales tax, property tax [p. 572]
10. Education   [p. 570]

True/False.

1. T [p. 565]	3. T [p. 554]	5. T [p. 563]	7. T [p. 565]	9. F [p. 572]
2. F [p. 552]	4. TF [p. 551]	6. T [p. 564]	8. T [p. 567]	10. F [p. 573]

Multiple-Choice.

1 c [p. 551]	6. a [p. 560]	11. b [p. 566]	16. c [p. 572]
2. c [p. 553]	7. c [p. 563]	12. d [p. 567]	17. a [p. 572]
3. b [p. 552]	8. a [p. 564]	13. c [p. 569]	18. b [p. 572]
4. b [p. 556]	9. c [p. 565]	14. d [p. 570]	19. b [p. 572]
5. d [p. 558]	10. d [p. 566]	15. c [p. 572]	20. d [p. 573]

Short Essay Answers

1. Discuss the provisions of direct democracy that many states allow in their constitution [p. 558-560].

    *   State constitutions allow direct democracy in initiative, referendum, and recall.
    *   Legislative initiative allows citizens to circulate a petition to place an issue on the ballot. A certain percentage of the registered voters in the last gubernatorial election are required to place the item on the ballot
    *   A referendum is similar to the initiative, except that the issue is proposed first by the legislature and then directed to the voters for their approval. This is most often used for local bond issues and amendments to state constitutions.
    *   Recall is the right of citizens to remove an elected official from office before their term has expired. Citizens must circulate petitions and get a certain number of signatures to place the recall on the ballot.

2. Explain the four major types of local government units [p. 563-565]. The four types of local governments are municipalities, counties, towns and townships, and special districts.

    -   Municipalities are a political entity created by people to govern themselves locally. Municipalities rely on financial assistance from state and national government.
    -   Counties are local governments set up as political extensions of state government. Counties apply state law and administer state business at the local level.
    -   Towns in New England states are governing units that combine the roles of city and county in one unit. The word town can be used as just another name for a city. The New England town is unique to that part of the country. Townships are somewhat like counties. Unlike New England towns, they are rural governments only.

3. Discuss the four general plans for governing municipalities [p. 566-568]. The four general plans are (1) the commission plan, (2) the council-manager plan, (3) the mayor-administrator plan, and (4) the mayor-council plan.

    -   The commission plan, which originated in Galveston, Texas, concentrates legislative and executive powers in the hands of city commissioners. Each commissioner is individually responsible for heading a particular city department. The mayor is one of the commissioners, and has only ceremonial powers.
    -   In the council-manager plan, the city council appoints a professional manager, who acts as chief executive. The mayor may be a member of the city council or not, but has only ceremonial powers.
    -   The mayor-administrator plan is often used in large cities where there is a strong mayor. The mayor appoints an administrative officer, whose function is to free the mayor from routine administrative tasks.
    -   The mayor-council plan is the oldest and most widely used. It consists of a mayor, who is an elected chief executive, and the city council is the legislative body. There are two sub-varieties, the weak mayor and the strong mayor. About 50 percent of American cities use some form of the mayor-council plan.

4. Examine the basic areas of revenues and expenditures for state and local government [p. 570-573]. Both state and local government spending are concentrated in the areas of education, public welfare, highways, health, and police protection. Education is the biggest category of spending. See Tables 18-3 and 18-4, p. 570.

    -   The most important tax revenue at the state level is the general sales tax. The property tax is the most important revenue source at the local level. Non-tax revenues include federal grants, publicly operated businesses, court fines, and increasingly state lotteries.
    -   In the 1980s and 1990s, with the national government shifting more responsibility to the states, state governments were having problems balancing their budgets. Two approaches were tried, increasing taxes, and reducing spending. Generally, the states that reduced spending, had better economic growth.